Gateways
To

HEAVEN

Published by:
Gita Publishing House
Sadhu Vaswani Mission,
10, Sadhu Vaswani Path,
Pune -411 001, (India).
gph@sadhuvaswani.org

Second Edition

ISBN : 978-93-80743-17-2

Printed by:
Mehta Offset Pvt. Ltd.
Mehta House,
A-16, Naraina Industrial Area II,
New Delhi-110 028, (India).
info@mehtaoffset.com

Gateways
To

HEAVEN

J.P. VASWANI

GITA PUBLISHING HOUSE
PUNE, (INDIA).
www.dadavaswanisbooks.org

OTHER BOOKS AND BOOKLETS BY DADA J.P. VASWANI

In English:
10 Commandments of A Successful Marriage
108 Pearls of Practical Wisdom
108 Simple Prayers of A Simple Man
108 Thoughts on Success
114 Thoughts on Love
A Little Book of Life
A Simple And Easy Way To God
A Treasure of Quotes
Around The Camp Fire
Begin The Day With God
Bhagavad Gita in a Nutshell
Burn Anger Before Anger Burns You
Daily Inspiration
Daily Inspiration (Booklet)
Destination Happiness
Dewdrops of Love
Does God Have Favourites?
Ecstasy and Experiences
Formula For Prosperity
God In Quest of Man
Good Parenting
Gurukul
Gurukul II
How To Overcome Depression
I am a Sindhi
In 2012 All Will Be Well
Joy Peace Pills
Kill Fear Before Fear Kills You
Ladder of Abhyasa
Lessons Life Has Taught Me
Life After Death
Management Moment by Moment
Mantras For Peace Of Mind
Many Paths: One Goal
Nearer, My God, To Thee!
New Education Can Make the World New
Peace or Perish
Positive Power of Thanksgiving
Questions Answered
Sadhu Vaswani : His Life And Teachings
Saints For You and Me
Saints With A Difference
Secrets of Health And Happiness
Shake Hand With Life
Short Sketches of Saints Known & Unknown
Sketches of Saints Known & Unknown
Stop Complaining: Start Thanking!
Swallow Irritation Before Irritation Swallows You
Teachers are Sculptors
The Goal Of Life and How To Attain It
The Little Book of Freedom From Stress
The Little Book of Prayer
The Little Book of Service
The Little Book of Success
The Little Book of Wisdom
The Little Book of Yoga
The Magic of Forgiveness
The Perfect Relationship: Guru and Disciple
The Seven Commandments of the Bhagavad Gita
The Terror Within
The Way of Abhyasa (How To Meditate)
Thus Have I Been Taught
Tips For Teenagers
What You Would Like To know About Karma
What You Would Like To know About Hinduism

What To Do When Difficulties Strike
Why Do Good People Suffer?
You Are Not Alone God Is With You!

Story Books:
101 Stories For You And Me
25 Stories For Children and also for Teens
It's All A Matter of Attitude
Snacks For The Soul
More Snacks For The Soul
Break The Habit
The Lord Provides
The Heart of a Mother
The King of Kings
The One Thing Needful
The Patience of Purna
The Power of Good Deeds
The Power of Thought
Trust Me All in All or Not at All
Whom Do You Love the Most
You Can Make A Difference

In Hindi:
Aalwar Santon Ki Mahan Gaathaayen
Atmik Jalpaan
Aapkay Karm, Aapkaa Bhaagy Banaatay Hein
Atmik Poshan
Bhakton Ki Uljhanon Kaa Saral Upaai
Bhale Logon Ke Saath Bura Kyon?
Dainik Prerna
Dar Se Mukti Paayen
Ishwar Tujhe Pranam
Jiski Jholi Mein Hain Pyaar
Krodh Ko Jalayen Swayam Ko Nahin
Laghu Kathayein
Mrutyu Hai Dwar… Phir Kya?
Nava Pushp (Bhajans In Hindi and Sindhi)
Prarthna ki Shakti
Pyar Ka Masiha
Sadhu Vaswani: Unkaa Jeevan Aur Shikshaayen
Safal Vivah Ke Dus Rahasya
Santon Ki Leela
Sri Bhagavad Gita:Gaagar Mein Saagar

In Marathi:
Krodhala Shaanth Kara, Krodhane Ghala Ghalnya
    Purvee (Burn Anger Before Anger Burns You)
Jiski Jholi Mein Hain Pyaar
Life After Death
Pilgrim of Love
Sind and the Sindhis
Sufi Sant (Sufi Saints of East and West)
What You Would Like To Know About Karma

Other Publications:

Recipe Books:
90 Vegetarian Sindhi Recipes
Di-li-cious Vegetarian Recipes
Simply Vegetarian

Books on Dada J. P. Vaswani:
A Pilgrim of Love
Dada J.P. Vaswani: His Life and Teachings
Dada J.P. Vaswani's Historic Visit to Sind
Dost Thou Keep Memory
How To Embrace Pain
Living Legend
Moments with a Master

CONTENTS

Preface

Gateways To Heaven was the title that came to mind, when it was decided to compile the brief, informal talks I had given to a few brothers and sisters, during my enforced period of rest and recuperation at the Rush Medical Centre in Chicago.

Gateways to Heaven is inspired directly by the *Yoga Vasishta* to which I have referred in my earlier books. The *Yoga Vasishta* written by Maharishi Valmiki is not well known among many of us. But it is a unique work, a work of wisdom incorporating Sage Vasishta's teachings to Sri Rama, in the form of a dialogue. For countless centuries it has inspired and guided spiritual seekers. In this brilliant treatise, Sage Vasishta describes *moksha* as a mansion with four gates, each one guarded by a gate keeper or sentry.

Who are these gatekeepers? *Satsanga, samattva, santosha* and *vichara* – good association, equanimity, contentment and spiritual reflection – these are described as the four "gatekeepers" of *mukti* or liberation in the *Yoga Vashishta*. They are also dynamic aids, we are told, in the cultivation of *sattva* or pure living.

If there is indeed a 'gateway' we had to pass through in order to reach Heaven, what are the 'entrance procedures' which will operate on us? And what kinds of gates are we talking about?

Sometime ago, a sister who has been fighting a life-long battle against over weight, remarked to me that she had decided to give a spiritual dimension to her diet regime. She put up a sticker on her fridge which read: *The Gates of Heaven are Narrow!*

I told her that she was closer to the truth than she imagined: for had not Jesus said to his followers: "It is easier for a camel to go through the eye of a needle than for a rich man to enter the Kingdom of God."

On a more serious note, the eye-of-the-needle metaphor suggests that the gates of Heaven are not a free-for-all passage allowing all comers to enter at will. Nor are there VIP passes or special bookings, nor any reservations, or free permits to cross the gates.

According to Hindu belief, Yama's brother and Chief Dispenser of Justice, Chitragupta, stands at the portals of heaven, and is in possession of that significant ledger wherein are maintained the most minute details of our 'credit' and 'debit' – in short, the good and bad *karmas* we have accumulated in this lifetime. *Jaise Karni Vaise Bharni* – as we sow, so we shall reap. "Go thou to the heaven or to the earth, according to thy merit…" so say our ancient scriptures.

What have we been up to, in our hectic lives? More pointedly, what exactly have we *done* with our lives? At the gates of heaven, we will face a moment of truth, a moment of reckoning, when we are forced to contemplate the answer to this deeply personal question. What is our deserving? What is our claim to merit?

If you are applying for a job, you can produce an impressive CV or bio-data, listing your academic achievements and your work experience.

If you are applying for a government license to start a new business, you can produce an impressive list of your assets and contacts and skills.

If you are looking to find a place for yourself in the Forbes Fortune 500, your bank accounts, your stocks and shares, your capital and movable/immovable properties will take you a long way.

But heaven is a different proposition! Your Ph.D., your BMW, your farmhouse, your MNC, your influence and your power are not going to open those gates for you! Heaven is really far more democratic, far more egalitarian than most of our countries on earth. We all have a free, fair and equal chance of making it across those sought-after gates.

If there are some among you who feel that you would rather linger on this earth for as long as possible, and would prefer not to think of heaven just yet, let me add for your benefit: this is not only about the gateway to heaven *after death*, it is also about the gateway to making life on earth a heaven!

J. P. Vaswani

• • • • • • • • • • • •

There is a path – the path of Light and Liberation – that will take us to the Abode of the Highest, from where none returns. It is the abode of the Supreme, the abode of *Brahman*, the Abode of the Eternal. Here, you will touch the plane of the pure white light, the radiance that casts no shadow, and you will be free, liberated from the cycle of birth and death.

J. P. Vaswani

• • • • • • • • • • • •

It's Beautiful!

John was an eleven-year-old patient who was dying of lymphoma. In his last days, he was hospitalised with severe, untreatable pneumonia. Though he was having difficulty breathing and was in constant pain, he was given very few drugs such as morphine and valium. Three days before John died, a circle of loved ones gathered around his bed. They were startled when John suddenly sat upright and announced that Jesus was in the room. He then asked for everyone to pray for him.

At about three a.m., John sat up again, startling the four people who had gathered around the bed to pray. "There are beautiful colours in the sky!" he shouted. "There are beautiful colours and more colours. You can double jump up here, double jump!"

By dawn, it seemed that life was almost over for John. His breathing was laboured, and his heart was pounding like that of a marathon runner's. Even then, little John had more to communicate. Opening his eyes wide, he asked his grieving parents to "let me go".

"Don't be afraid," he said. "I've seen God, angels, and shepherds. I see the white horse." As sick as he was, John still begged his family not to feel sorry for him. He had seen where he was going, and it was a joyous and wondrous place. "It's wonderful. It's beautiful," he said, his hand held out in front of him. Soon he laid back and fell asleep. John never regained consciousness and died two days later.

From *Glimpses of Heaven*, Aurora Production, AG

WHAT IS HEAVEN?

The English word heaven was originally derived from a term of reference to the sky or firmament. As time passed, it assumed a deeper philosophical meaning as a state of after-life; subsequently, it came to refer to the place where God dwells. Although there are as many different concepts of heaven as there are different religious faiths, I must say the opposite of heaven, i.e. hell, has pretty much the same connotation across all religious distinctions: whether they are Hindus, Christians or Muslims, people will agree that hell is a state or a place where God is absent.

> **We shall not rest from our work but from our labours. There will be no toil, no pain in the work.**
> *-Anonymous*

To the Chinese, heaven is a place where ancestors reside. However Mozi, the Chinese scholar, takes a more theistic view, regarding Heaven as a seat of Sovereign Power with Divine ordinance over the earth. He writes in his book, *Will of Heaven*:

"I know Heaven loves men dearly not without reason. Heaven ordered the sun, the moon and the stars to enlighten and guide them. Heaven ordained the four seasons, spring, autumn, winter and summer, to regulate them. Heaven sent down snow, frost, rain, and dew to grow the five grains and flax and silk so that the people could use and enjoy them. Heaven established the hills and rivers, ravines and valleys, and arranged many things to minister to man's good or bring him evil. He

> # Heaven is not all rest. On the door is inscribed: 'No admission except on business'.
> *-Anonymous*

appointed the dukes and lords to reward the virtuous and punish the wicked, and to gather metal and wood, birds and beasts, and to engage in cultivating the five grains and flax and silk to provide for the people's food and clothing. This has been so from antiquity to the present."

In the Gospel according to Matthew, we read:

"Again, the Kingdom of heaven is like unto treasure hid in a field; which when a man hath found, he hideth, and for joy thereof, goeth and selleth all that he hath, and buyeth that field." (Matthew 13:44)

Luke offers a more subtle definition:

"The Kingdom of God does not come visibly, nor will people say, 'Here it is,' or 'There it is,' because the Kingdom of God is within you." (Luke: 17:20-21)

In Islam, the state of blessed afterlife is referred to as paradise; according to the Holy Quran, paradise is a beautiful garden, where the chosen few will reside in eternal bliss:

"Verily for the righteous there will be a fulfillment of (the heart's) desires; gardens enclosed, and grapevines; companions of equal age; and a cup full (to the brim). No vanity shall they hear therein, nor untruth: recompense from thy Lord, a gift, (amply) sufficient..." (Sura 78:31-36)

> # You grow to heaven. You don't go to heaven.
> ## - Edgar Cayce

According to Roman Catholic belief, Heaven is the Realm of the Blessed Trinity of Father, Son and Holy Spirit, as also the home of the Blessed Virgin Mary, who is known as the Queen of Heaven; it is a place where the angels and the saints reside. The essential joy of heaven is called the beatific vision, which is the ultimate bliss derived from the vision of God's essence. In this heaven, the soul rests perfectly in God, and does not, or cannot desire anything else than God.

In the Protestant faith, true believers get to spend eternity with God, and with other good souls like themselves. 'Heaven' will be the place where life will be lived to the full, in the way that God intended, each believer 'loving the Lord their God with all their heart and with all their soul and with all their mind' and 'loving their neighbour as themselves'; it is a place of great joy, without any of the negative aspects of earthly life.

The word paradise actually derives from the ancient Persian language, where it means a walled garden or park, and religious scholars say that it was Zoroastrianism that first gave us notions of the afterlife that were adopted or modified by the later Abrahamaic religions. Zoroastrianism offers us an interesting perspective, because, unlike many other religions, it claims that everyone will eventually get into heaven, though it might take a while. The paradise of Zoroastrianism is attained by crossing the Bridge of the Separator, which widens when the righteous approach it.

> # Heaven would be a very hell to a wicked person.
> ### -David Berg

In Hinduism *moksha* (the Sanskrit term for liberation) or *mukti* (release) is considered far superior to heaven, which at best, can only give us rewards for all the good we have done; when we have reaped the fruit of all our good *karma*, we must go back to re-enter the cycle of birth and death. Far superior to heaven or *swarga* is *moksha*, the ultimate liberation from the cycle of death and rebirth.

For most Hindus, *moksha* is the highest goal. It means liberation and release from the world of *samsara*, the eternal cycle of birth, suffering, death, and rebirth. It is a state of union with God.

From the root meaning of the English word, 'heaven' to the ultimate goal of *mukti* or *moksha:* we have explored many versions, many aspects of the state of bliss which we refer to as heaven. What I wish to talk about is that highly desired, much sought after state of *sat chit ananda* which is achieved only when we attain to the Lotus Feet of the Lord. Although we pursue other goals in life, although it is not possible for us to shake off our worldly cares and concerns just like that, my plea is that we must never, ever lose sight of this ultimate

> # The best way to get to heaven is to take it with you.
> *-Henry Drummond*

goal. The seven gateways that I shall talk about in the following pages will not only lead you to the ultimate goal, but will also ensure that your life upon this earth is blessed and fulfilled in every way – in short, heavenly, for you and those around you.

· · · · · · · · · · · · ·

I would describe compassion as the crown of all virtues. I believe it is this quality that takes us closest to the Divine within each one of us. When we practise — not just feel — compassion, when we go out of ourselves to reach out to others and alleviate their suffering, we rise to the Highest Self in us. Need I say that at such times, negative feelings of strife and disharmony are totally nullified in our hearts and minds? And when more and more of us practise the divine quality of compassion, will our world not move towards lasting peace?

J. P. Vaswani

· · · · · · · · · · · · ·

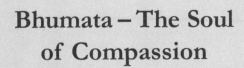

Bhumata – The Soul of Compassion

There is a legend told to us about the Third *Avatara* of Lord Vishnu, namely, the *Varaha Avatara*. As we know, the Lord assumed the shape of a Divine Boar to rescue *Bhumata* or Mother Earth, who was none other than His own Consort, worshipped by the faithful as Bhoomi Devi. Plunging into the depths of the oceans (remember, there was no earth then, for *Bhumata* had fled in fear from the *rakshasas* (evil demons) who wished to capture her), he found Bhoomi Devi and effortlessly carried her to the surface, perched safely on his snout. The *devas* and the gods watched in rapture and devotion as they beheld the Lord's Divine Form, with His consort safely ensconced near his very eyes.

Well, the story goes that as Lord Vishnu looked at His Divine spouse with love, he saw her shedding tears!

"Do not weep, Beloved," he said to her. "Did you imagine that I would fail to rescue you? Don't you know that I could never be parted from you? Are you not aware that all this is part of my Divine *leela*?"

"No, my Lord," said Bhumata. "I was certain that you would indeed come to my rescue. I weep not for myself, but for the generations to come upon this earth. Oh tell me, will you save them from the ocean of sin and despair with the same love and concern with which you rushed to my aid?"

"Truly, you are the personification of *Daya*, the very embodiment of compassion," the Lord said to Her. "And I promise you, I will rush to the rescue of every soul with the same promptitude as I have done now!"

This beautiful legend emphasis something very important—the power of compassion, which is a divine attribute.

CHAPTER

2

THE FIRST GATEWAY TO

HEAVEN:

COMPASSION

Compassion is indeed the crown of all virtues. Compassion is closely linked to all the cardinal virtues. It arises out of Love and Charity. It is the basis of *seva* or service. Truth, I regard as one of the gateways to Heaven; and the truth of truths is Compassion! *Daya Dharma Kaa Mool Hai!*

My Master, Sadhu Vaswani, who was verily a Messiah of compassion, put it in admirable words: "Service of the poor is worship of God."

> ## Compassion is the key to the doors of Divine Grace.
> *-Swami Ramalingam*

Is not service the best form of worship? And is not compassion the very root, the fountainhead of service?

The philosophical foundation of compassion in Hinduism is rooted in the Vedantic ideal of the One Life in All Creation. "All that is, is a vesture of the Lord," proclaims the *Isa Upanishad*. The concept of the Brahman, or Universal Soul, encompasses the entirety of existence. Since all aspects of existence are part of this Universal Soul, Hindus believe that the Divine is manifested in every living being. This leads to the ideal of Reverence for all life, and its corollary, *daya* or compassion, and *ahimsa* or non-violence.

The concept of compassion is also central to Buddhism. For the Buddha taught that human beings are afflicted with various kinds of *dukha* or sufferings, associated with old age, sickness, death, grief, pain and despair — and the spirit of compassion is what we require to wipe out human suffering to the best extent possible.

Christianity, too, regards compassion as a blessed quality. "Blessed are the merciful," Jesus said. "for they shall obtain mercy."

Islamic scholars tell us that compassion is central to Islam — in fact, it represents the true spirit of Islam. The names *Rahman* and *Rahim* (The Compassionate, the Merciful) are the names by which every devout Muslim invokes Allah in his daily prayers.

Dear friends, *talking* about compassion is not what we need today! My purpose in citing these various scriptures is only to show that all major religions of the world lay emphasis on compassion—compassion in thought, word and action!

There is a parable that tells us of a mother with paralysed arms, who saw her child being swept away along the fast moving currents of a river, but was unable to do anything to save the child. This illustrates the fact that *feeling* is not enough—we have to act; we must find the means and ways to relieve others' suffering and pain—this is *meaningful* compassion.

Many of us are ready to love and sympathise with those who are close to us—relatives, friends, loved ones. We may go out of our way to help them—but when strangers are involved, do we rush to their help, or do we simply turn away? *This* is the true test of compassion.

> **Can we not cultivate in our children and in ourselves a vast compassion? This compassion will make us eager to know the sorrows of all men, the griefs of our land and the dangers to which in these modern days the religion is exposed; and this growing knowledge will produce strong workers, working for work's sake, ready to die, if only they may serve their country and fellow-men.**
>
> *-Sister Nivedita*

Some of us are ever willing to help our fellow human beings—but what about animals? How many of us kill animals to nourish our own lives? How can this be reconciled with true compassion?

The greatest form of compassion can only come by understanding the central concept of *Vedanta* of which I spoke earlier – namely, that all life is one. The life that sleeps in stones and minerals, the life that stirs in plants and trees, the life that dreams in animals and birds is the same life that awakes and breathes in man. And this life is the very spark of the Life Universal.

I am sure Aung San Syu Kyi needs no introduction to you. This remarkable and courageous woman became the leader of the democratic movement in Burma. Placed under house arrest by the military regime, she was awarded the Nobel Prize for Peace in 1991. Here is what she has to say about compassion in the context of world peace:

> The essential distinction between savages and civilised men lies not in differences of dress, dwelling, food, deportment or possessions—but in the way we treat our fellow human beings. It is the degree of humanity in our relationship with others that decides how far we have travelled from a state of savagery towards an ideal world of civilised beings who truly have learnt the art of peaceful co-existence.

There are many ways of defining humanity. I would like to define it in terms of *bodhi-chitta*—the mind of enlightenment. Those filled with both compassion and wisdom add greatly to the positive civilised forces of the world by combating savage passions that urge men to inflict suffering on their fellow human beings.

Compassion without wisdom is ineffective; wisdom without compassion is soulless. When a compassionate heart is linked to an insightful mind, then we can make a significant contribution to peace upon this earth.

Gurudev Sadhu Vaswani once narrated to us a story of the seeker, who wanted to learn the secret of the Life Beautiful. It was taught to him by an old man, whose face was radiant with the light of joy and peace. The old man said to the seeker, "From morn till night I seek to serve. I am busy, busy, working for others, trying to help others, trying to serve the poor, sending out my sympathy and love to those who stand in need of help and strength, serving them in this broken world."

The young seeker was thrilled. Suddenly, this discovery shone within his heart – that the others were not apart from him, but a part of himself. "They are mine, as I am theirs," he said to himself. "No separation between me and the poor and suffering ones, between me and the lowly ones! We are one! We are brothers!"

Thus did he discover the secret of the Life Beautiful, which was nothing but sympathy and compassion that went out to all. Henceforth, he would give out love and compassion to all, and his would be the Life Beautiful.

Once Gandhiji and Kasturba were visiting a village. While Gandhiji was busy talking to the men, Ba went among the women and spoke to them of cleanliness and personal hygiene. "You must bathe everyday," she told them earnestly, "and change into clean, washed clothes."

> **Is there a nobler name and a nobler offering than compassion – *Maitri?* The modern age, dominated by machinery and materialism, may yet be saved by the spirit of Compassion and Love, which has inspired the noblest philosophers, literatures, arts and idealisms of the East.**
>
> *-Sadhu Vaswani*

A poor woman took Ba into her hut and said to her, "Ba, the only clothes I have are these which I'm wearing now. How can I change clothes and wash them daily?"

Ba was profoundly moved by the woman's plight. She spoke of the incident to Gandhiji later that day.

"What can we do for them?" she asked him in anguish.

During those days Gandhiji used to wear the traditional Indian clothes: *dhoti*, *kurta, angavastra* and turban. Forthwith he decided that he would wear only a loincloth from then on, for so many of his brothers and sisters had no clothes on their backs!

Such an awareness, such compassion, such a sensitivity came to Gurudev Sadhu Vaswani too, when he was a child. Sometimes, as he sat down to his meals and heard the cry of a passing beggar, he would take away his food to share it with the hungry one. From the beginning of his days, he was filled with the spirit of compassion for all who were in suffering and pain.

Again and again, his mother found him awake in the middle of cold, wintry nights.

"What keeps you awake, my child?" she would ask him. "Is it the cold of the winter? Then let me wrap around you one more blanket or quilt."

He said to her, "Mother, the cold I feel cannot be overcome by a hundred blankets or quilts!"

"I do not understand you, my child," said the mother. "Speak to me in plain words, not riddles!"

He said, "Mother, I am thinking of hundreds of homeless ones who, in this severe cold, are lying on the roadside. Their cold seems to pierce my frame."

Throughout his life, Gurudev Sadhu Vaswani had this sense of identification with the poor and destitute. In later years, once when he was ill, he was unable to take solid food. He felt that he would like to taste an orange. Several oranges were brought to him. As he looked at them, his thoughts moved out to the sick people who lay in the poor patients' wards of the Government Hospital. Without tasting a single orange himself, he sent them all to the poor patients. And he said, "I feel satisfied. I feel as though I have eaten all the oranges!"

Many said to him, "When you give to the poor, you do not discriminate, you do not make sure if the person to whom you give is deserving or otherwise."

Gurudev Sadhu Vaswani said, "The Lord gives without hesitation to an undeserving person like me. Who am I to enquire into the deserts of other?"

On one occasion, Gurudev Sadhu Vaswani said in good humour, "The man who gives only to those whom he considers deserving has reason to pray that the Lord, in judging him, will not follow his example."

When we give of ourselves, of our time and our wealth, we must learn to give in the right spirit, the spirit of true compassion, for "the gift without the giver is bare", as the famous saying goes.

A special collection was being made for earthquake victims during a public discourse by a religious leader. As the collection box was brought to him, a wealthy man said to the volunteer, "Here's ten dollars. I thank God I can give it away and not feel it!"

The volunteer advised him gently, "In that case brother, make it twenty dollars and feel it! The blessing really comes, when you feel it!"

> Some folks give their mite,
> Others give with their might,
> And some don't give who might
> What we give, we must give as an offering to God.

A wealthy man was approached by a charitable organisation for a donation. "I'll give my mite," said the prosperous merchant, as he drew out a single currency note from his wallet carefully.

"Do you mean the widow's mite, by any chance?" enquired the volunteer.

"Why, yes!" laughed the merchant. "It is not how much I give that matters. That is the widow's mite, isn't it?"

"I will be satisfied with half that much," replied the volunteer. "May I ask you how much you are worth?"

"Oh, about fifty lakhs," said the merchant.

"Then just give me twenty-five lakhs," said the volunteer. "That will be just half the widow's mite, for she gave all that she had!"

During his brief stay at Jamshedpur, Gurudev Sadhu Vaswani presided over a meeting at which an appeal was made for the famine-stricken ones. Gurudev Sadhu Vaswani's speech touched the secret chord of compassion in many hearts. A rich man came forward with a donation of a thousand rupees. The announcement was received with an applause. Many others offered their contributions. A poor old woman came to Gurudev Sadhu Vaswani and, placing in his hand two copper coins, said, "This is all I have, Master! And I give it to you to be used as you like."

Some laughed at the old woman. One of the organiser said to Gurudev Sadhu Vaswani, "Of what use will these two copper coins be to us? May we not return them to old woman?"

Gurudev Sadhu Vaswani valued the old woman's gift, for he knew that the two copper coins were given with true compassion. He said, "These copper coins are of value in the sight of Him who sees beyond appearances. He gazes into the heart! We applaud outer acts, God sees the interior motives!"

It has wisely been said: Giving is living! For the health of the human body depends on its exhalations as well its inhalations. It is reported that a young boy, who was to don the role of a shining angel, was covered with a coating of fine gold leaf. The coating closed all the pores of his skin, and he died as a consequence of this disastrous make-up.

This must serve as a warning to all of us, who have the tendency to cover ourselves with our wealth! Let not the pores of our compassion, benevolence and generosity be clogged by wealth! Let us not be constrained to die a spiritual death, smothered in the wealth of this world!

All that we give, in love and compassion, we give to the Lord Himself. The first beneficiary of such service is not the receiver, but the giver – for it takes him closer to the Lord.

There was a girl, who had achieved this closeness to the Lord. She was the only daughter of a very wealthy man. She was young and beautiful – the kind of girl young men would turn to look at admiringly. But she was a special human being. She devoted her time to service in a lepers' colony.

Everyday she went to work there. She nursed and cared for the leprosy victims lovingly and carefully; she cleansed their sores which oozed with foul smelling pus; tenderly, she dressed their wounds; she served food to them and fed those who could not use their hands.

One day a friend of her father happened to visit the colony. He was taken aback at the sight of the young girl. Here was an exquisite creature, so young, so beautiful and bubbling with life and vitality! She seemed to enjoy spending her life in the service of those people whom their families had abandoned.

The visitor could not contain his feelings.

"How could you bring yourself to do this?" he asked her. "I wouldn't do this even if I were offered a million rupees!"

The girl smiled. "I wouldn't do this for all the money in the world either!" she said.

Gently pointing to the pendant of Lord Krishna which she wore around her neck, she added, "I do it for *His* sake."

Her compassion was rooted in *bhakti* – devotion to the Lord.

Once, a saint was bathing in a river. All of a sudden his eyes fell on a scorpion which was being drowned in the water. Moved by compassion, the saint picked up the scorpion and saved it. The scorpion bit him and while doing so fell back into the river. Although the scorpion bite was very painful, the saint made a second attempt to retrieve the scorpion from the water. Again the scorpion bit him and as the saint wrung his hand in pain the scorpion fell into the water yet again. The saint did not give up; but when he picked the scorpion from the water for the third time, he left it on the dry bank of the river. A man watching this scene approached the saint and said, "Wasn't one scorpion bite enough for you, that you repeated this process several times?" The saint gently replied, "It is in the nature of the scorpion to bite. The scorpion does not change its behaviour. It is in my nature to be kind and compassionate. If the scorpion does not change its behaviour, then why should I? Irrespective of others' behaviour, it is my nature to love one and all. To me all the creatures are an image of God. To love them is my *dharma*."

Jeedhar Dekhta Hoon Udhar Tu Hi Tu Hai,
Ke Har Shae Mein Jalwa Tera Hu-bahoo Hai !

Wherever I turn, O Lord, I see none but You! Every sight, every object is a reflection of Your radiant beauty!

If anyone hurts us, creates obstacles and knowingly troubles us, we should change our perception and consider these people as an image of God and forgive and forget their behaviour. That is the way to experience true peace.

George Washington and Peter Miller were classmates. Both were fast friends. Time changed their lives, and took them on different paths. George Washington became the President of America and Peter Miller became a devotee of the Lord.

Now, Peter Miller had an enemy by the name of Michael Whitman. It often happens that some people create obstacles in the way of good work. Possessed as they are by a demon, they try to let down the good people. For twenty long years Michael harassed Peter Miller. Both of them had been involved in the war of American independence. But Michael proved to be a traitor. He was sent to the gallows and was sentenced to death. Michael could ask for reprieve by appealing to the head of the State. But he had no one to plead his case.

Peter Miller, who had always been harassed and ill-treated by Michael, felt compassion for him. He knew that the death sentence could be revoked by the President of the country and the President happened to be George Washington, who was his childhood friend and classmate. The office of the President was seventy miles away from Peter's residence. He had no means of transport. He walked seventy miles to meet the President and request him for the reprieve of the death sentence on Michael.

George Washington was very happy to meet his friend Peter. "Tell me, what can I do for you?" he said, after exchanging pleasantries and welcoming him with warmth and affection. Peter replied, "George, for the sake of our friendship, you will have to do me a favour. I know you love me a lot. It is this love which makes me plead for revocation of the death sentence on Michael Whitman."

George Washington was surprised. "Peter, how can I forgive a traitor? He has committed a great crime. I am sorry. I cannot help your friend. Michael will have to suffer capital punishment. It is impossible for me to forgive Michael."

Peter continued to plead, "You are mistaken, Michael is not my friend. He has been my enemy for the last twenty years.

He has always opposed me in every venture I have undertaken."

"Then forget all about it," Washington said. "The question of forgiving him does not arise, since he is your worst enemy."

Peter apprised George about the various ways in which Michael had harassed him. In spite of all that Peter said that he had walked seventy miles especially to appeal for him. Listening to him George Washington was profoundly moved. He said, "If you can forgive your worst enemy and plead for him, it is the Almighty Lord who Himself is pleading for Michael's forgiveness. I agree to your request and repeal the death sentence."

It requires the utmost compassion to love your enemies and forgive those who have ill-treated you.

"Love, love, love even thine enemy," said Gurudev Sadhu Vaswani, "and though he hate thee as a thorn, thou wilt blossom as a rose!"

Gurudev Sadhu Vaswani always returned love for hate. "Why do you do so?" he was asked. Quietly, he answered, "Each man gives what he has. God has given me nothing but love!"

One of his associates had greatly wronged Gurudev Sadhu Vaswani just because his niece was not appointed as the Head of the Mira School. He wrote a number of falsehoods against Gurudev Sadhu Vaswani and his organisation in the newspaper, purchased copies of the same and distributed them free among many of those who attended Gurudev's *satsang*. Gurudev was silent. He spoke not a word in self-defence.

After a few years, the man realised the grievous fault he had committed. He came and fell at Gurudev's feet and, weeping like a child, said, "You are a true Saint of God! I am a sinner. I spread falsehoods against you. Not once did you utter a word against me. Pray forgive this repentant sinner and tell me what I may do to repent."

Gurudev lifted him up and, folding him in a warm embrace said, "Weep not, brother. If you would repent aright, forget all that you have done – and remember God!"

The essential quality of his life, as it has seemed to me, through the many years that it had been my undeserved privilege to be near him, was his divine compassion and tenderness for all those whom the cruel world tramples upon day after day. I was with him during the few days that he was sent to the Karachi Jail for having launched a *Satyagraha* campaign for a socio-religious cause. I saw with what tenderness he met thieves and murderers, sinners and criminals. On learning that a man of God was their fellow 'guest', they came to him, they beheld in his eyes the light of a brother, and they opened out their hearts to him, making a clear confession of the crimes they had committed. And often their eyes and the eyes of Gurudev Sadhu Vaswani glistened with unbidden tears. "They are my friends and brothers," Gurudev said to me. "And to them I fain would reveal the boundless love and mercy of God."

Deep in his heart, there was the conviction that there is neither sin nor sinner. There is only God and His manifestations, His children, standing at different stages of evolution, all struggling to reach the Goal. "There is a treasure God giveth in darkness, and sinners are nearer to the Kingdom of Love than the self-righteous," he said. His daily prayer was radiant with the following moving words:

> O Lord! Have mercy on them whom men have made criminals by denying them work and bread and then, in their hunger and humiliation, have chained them in jails!

> O Lord! Dry the tears of them whom humanity hath not heeded and hath made harlots, too weak to resist the tempter and the tyrant!

His compassion was not restricted to human beings. It extended to all creatures, even to trees and flowers. He would not pluck flowers, for flowers, as he said, had their families, and they must not be separated from each other. So he did not accept flower-garlands. The quality of his soul was clearly revealed, also, in his treatment of animals. He could not resign himself to the sufferings of animals at the cruel hands of the butcher. "For me not to love bird and animal would be not to love the Lord," he said. "For His children are birds and animals, no less than human beings."

In the compound of St. Mira's High School was a shed; it was the dwelling place of a few lambs and goats, a cow and cocks rescued by Gurudev Sadhu Vaswani from the jaws of death as they were being driven to the slaughter house. "No price is too great to save a single life!" he said to me once. It was on such occasions that his large crystal eyes sparkled with a light which is not seen on land or sea. And, as I looked into the depths of that wondrous light, I had involuntarily exclaimed, "Are you Sadhu Vaswani or are you God?"

Have you read St. Paul's first Epistle to the Corinthians? It is part of the New Testament – but to my mind, it belongs to the religion of humanity. I regard it as one of the most inspiring passages which outlines the essential virtues for a happy and useful life. Here is a gist of that beautiful letter which the saint wrote to his loyal and devout followers:

> Love, compassion, charity, doing things for others – these are the essential qualities. Love never fails. Other things fade and pass away, but love endures. Faith, hope and love – these three endure. And the greatest of these is love.

Loving and giving – these have been regarded as the highest virtues. Let us remember too, Kahlil Gibran's words: "You give but little when you give of your possessions. It is when you give of yourself that you truly give."

The Bhagavad Gita tells us: "He who eats what is left from the sacrifice, is released from all sins: but the impious one, who cooks food for himself alone, he verily eats sin!"

Once upon a time, in this ancient land of ours, it was a practice among all people to share their food with others; kings and aristocrats performed *anna daana* as a matter of daily habit; the ordinary householders shared their food with guests; they also offered food to ascetics and beggars who came to their doorstep seeking alms; even beggars shared their food with birds and animals. But today, people store even a tiny roll of left-over dough in the fridge and save it for the next meal. Whatever food remains after the meal is 'locked' and 'stored' in airtight containers and put away in the fridge.

If you ask me, the fridge is a 'culprit' which prevents us from following the message of the Gita. The Gita tells us to share our food with others; the Gita also warns us that stale, left-over, reheated, old food is *tamasic*. On both counts, we would do well to give away any food that we may have in excess. But what do we see nowadays? There are no guests, no ascetics, no alms-seekers whom we are obliged to feed; all the food which otherwise would have been given away to the hungry, or to birds and stray dogs and cows, is stored in the fridge instead.

I must admit that I am often saddened when I see food being taken out of the fridge – for my heart pleads for those starving and hungry ones, who could have gratefully eaten the excess food preserved in the refrigerator.

Gurudev Sadhu Vaswani shared his food with the underprivileged every day. Before he sat down for lunch, he would take a portion of his meal and personally go out and give it to a beggar on the road.

Is this not the very essence of healthy living – sharing whatever we have with those who need it? For we must never ever forget that everything we possess, all that we have and hold, is left with us in the capacity of a trust. Sharing what we have with others brings joy and sublimates the mind. It fills man with the joy of expansion; it purifies him and 'detaches' him from the vice-like grip of 'absolute ownership'.

Very often, our 'compassion' is born of selfish motives. For example, when people leave the temple, they will ritualistically drop coins into the bowls of beggars lined up outside. This completes their visit to the temple, and they believe they gain *punya* from this act of charity. But the same people will turn their face away from beggars who accost them in public places. Some of them even reproach the poor beggars: "Aren't you ashamed of begging?" or "Why don't you find some useful employment?"

The man of true compassion gives without judgement. He never ever asks if the others deserve his charity or compassion.

Dr. W. Beran Wolfe was a young psychiatrist. Many men and women, who came to him for treatment – bitter, frightened, paranoid, anguished and frustrated – had been desperately unhappy, expecting him to provide a miracle cure which would help them achieve a tranquil adjustment to life.

Dr. Wolfe's compassion went out to those anguished people who had come to him for help. Young as he was, he realized that many of his patients were unhappy because they were obsessed with themselves. They had one trait in common: a totally selfish concept of life. Selfishly absorbed in their own interests and concerns, they had failed in human relationships; they had created their own unhappiness.

Dr. Wolfe realised that he had to make people understand that true happiness could not be found in *being* or *having,* but rather in doing – doing things with and for others. Thus was born his wonderful book, *How To Be Happy Though Human.* Let me quote a few lines from his book:

For those who seek the larger happiness and the greater effectiveness open to human beings, there can be but one philosophy of life, the philosophy of constructive altruism…the good life demands a working philosophy of active philanthropy as an orientating map of conduct. This is the golden way of life. This is the satisfying life. This is the way to be happy, though human.

> **Compassion is a sense of *shared* suffering, most often combined with a desire to *alleviate* the suffering, to show special *kindness* to those who suffer. Thus compassion is essentially *empathy,* but with an active slant indicating that the compassionate person will actually seek to aid those they feel for.**
> *-Anon.*

A beautiful story is told to us about Hussain, the martyr of Karbala. Once he was sitting at his dinner, and a slave was present to serve him. By an accident a hot dish fell on Hussain's knees.

The slave was terrified and recited a verse from the Holy Qur'an, "Paradise belongs to him who restrains his anger."

Hussain answered, "I am not angry."

The slave continued, "Paradise belongs to him who forgiveth his brother."

And Hussain said, "I forgive you!"

And the slave finished the verse, "For God loves the benevolent."

Immediately, Hussain responded, "I give you liberty! No longer are you my slave: and I give you four hundred pieces of silver!"

Truly, God loves men of compassion, God loves those who forgive their fellow men!

Ishwarah sarvabhutanaam hriddhes arjuna tisthathi, Sri Krishna teaches us in the Gita. "The Lord dwelleth in the heart of all beings, O Arjuna!"

How can we walk the way of true compassion? So let me offer you these practical suggestions:

1. Compassion begins in awareness. The first step on the path of compassion is to be aware that the One Life flows in all.

2. The second step of compassion is the acknowledgement that all Creation is One family; all the people of the world,

nay, even birds and animals are my younger brothers and sisters in the One family of Creation.

3. Compassion begins in awareness; but it is not enough to feel compassion, or express compassion through speech. Compassion should be expressed in action, in deeds of daily life, in little acts of kindness and love.

4. Selective compassion is selfish compassion! It is not enough to be kind and loving to those who are close to you, those whom you love, or those whom you consider your own. True compassion knows no barriers of caste, creed, race or faith. It falls like the gentle rain on all of humanity, all of creation.

5. Compassion is not giving of your money and your assets: true compassion is giving your love, giving yourself in an endless stream of sympathy that flows out to all.

6. Compassion is a divine attribute, and takes you closer to God. Therefore, compassion should be non-judgemental, and offered freely. When you begin to wonder whether people are worthy of your compassion, you are guilty of the kind of discrimination which even God does not practise against us, his erring children. Let the quality of your mercy be the determining factor in your acts of compassion – not the recipient's deserving.

If we are indeed God's children, made in His likeness, coming from Him and destined to return to His abode, His Lotus Feet, then we also need to cultivate qualities that are worthy of His children. We may not aspire to His power or His wisdom: but we can and must aspire to the one divine quality that we can all emulate; the quality of Mercy; the spark of Compassion which binds us to our fellow human beings and takes us closer to God Himself.

God is all Love. God is all Wisdom. He expects us to live and work not merely for our own pleasure and our own benefit, but also for the service and benefit of others. Is it not more blessed to *give* than to receive?

Compassion does not require a hefty wallet, strong limbs or heroic deeds or great and austere sacrifices.

A helping hand, a friendly word or gesture, a kind smile will more than suffice! And let me add, in the words of Mark Twain: "Kindness is a language which the deaf can hear and the blind can read!"

Compassion binds the world together in the bond of unity and peace. In the words of the Buddha: "In separateness lies the world's great misery, in compassion lies the world's true strength."

Daya dharma ka mool hai: compassion is the very soul, the very essence of religion. In the immortal words of Sant Tulsidas:

> *Daya Dharama ka mool hai, paap mool abhimaan,*
> *Tulsi daya na chhodieye, jab lag ghat mein praan.*
>
> Compassion is the very root of religion, even as pride is the root of sin;
> Let us be kind, let us practise compassion till the very last breath of our being.

Who is a true *bhakta*, a true devotee of the Lord? *Vaishnav Jan To Tene Kahiye, Je Peer Parayi Jane Re…* "You call that person as a true Vaishnav, who feels the pain of others," sings the saint of Gujarat, Narsi Mehta. A Jewish teacher tells us: "Kindness gives to *another*. Compassion knows no *'other'*." The great Jain tradition of non-violence is rooted in the virtue of compassion. The Buddhist scriptures tell us the story of Ananda, asking the Master, "Would it be true to say that the cultivation of loving kindness and compassion is a part of our practice?" To which the Buddha replied, "No. It would *not* be true to say that the cultivation of loving kindness and compassion is *part* of our practice. It would be true to say that the cultivation of loving kindness and compassion is *all* of our practice."

Compassion, kindness, loving mercy must be the tune, the theme, the very soul of the song we all sing together; it must be the great value that binds humanity together; the great value that we must pass on to our children and our children's children. Compassion is the answer to all our unanswered questions, the solution to humanity's stifling, suffocating problems: compassion to all living beings; compassion to our friends and family as well as our so-called foes and adversaries; compassion to all of creation; compassion to the tiniest creature that breathes the breath of life; when we have imbibed this great virtue into our lives and hearts, how can we allow violence, killing, slaughter of animals? How can we give in to destructive forces like terrorism? How can we allow differences between rich and poor, black and white, Asian and African, American and European, Hindu and Muslim, Sikh and Christian?

And so let me end with the beautiful Vedic prayer:

Sarve Bhavantu Sukhinah:
Sarve Santu Niramaya:
Sarve Badhrani Pashyantu
Maa Kashchid-Dukha Bhavbhaveta!

May all beings be happy,
May all be healthy,
May people have the well-being of all in mind,
May nobody suffer in any way.

• • • • • • • • • • • •

God is Truth and God is Love.
In your dealings with others,
bear witness to Truth.
And never forget that the Truth of
truths is Love, is Compassion.
Give the service of love to all.

J.P. Vaswani

• • • • • • • • • • •

The Triumph of Truth

The story of King Harishchandra is narrated in several of our ancient texts and *Puranas*. We are told that this story gave courage and hope to Yudhishtira, when the Pandavas were exiled to live in the forest for twelve years; in more recent times, Mahatma Gandhi is said to have been greatly inspired by the story of the King, who valued Truth above all else. There are different versions of the story from different sources: but the basic moral remains constant in all versions: to follow the way of truth is *dharma*; to yield to untruth is *adharma*.

It is said that the starting point of this story was in Indraloka, where the great saints and sages of yore were discussing the best way to *mukti* or liberation. While many exemplary virtues and ideals were put forward by the wise souls in the heaven world, Sage Vashishta was emphatic in upholding *satya vadana* – adherence to Truth – as the cardinal virtue essential to the life of *dharma*. He added that King Harishchandra was the very embodiment of this virtue, and that if the King were ever to swerve from the truth, he, sage Vashishta, would renounce all claims to sanctity and virtue. Hearing this, Sage Vishwamitra announced that he would indeed put Harishchandra to the test: if the King was found wanting, Vashishta would lose his position of prominence among the sages; on the other hand, if the king proved worthy of the good name bestowed on him, then Sage Vishwamitra would bestow the power of one half of his *taposhakti* on him, and bless the king, his progeny and his people with peace and prosperity.

The terms were agreed and testing times began for the monarch, whose life had always borne witness to the ideal of *satya*. One day, when he was out hunting, the king heard a woman's cry, deep in the forest: the voice cried out, "Help, oh help me! I am being molested by evildoers!" Hearing the forlorn cry, the king rushed towards the direction of the voice, with his raised sword. What he actually found there was the Sage Vishwamitra in his *tapasya*. The whole event had been deliberately planned by the sage to start his trial of the king's virtue.

Feigning anger, the sage was about to pronounce a curse on the king, when Harishchandra fell at his feet and offered his humble apologies to the *rishi*, for having disturbed him.

"What can you offer me in recompense for this grievous offence?" the sage demanded of him.

Without hesitation, the king offered to give the sage whatever he wanted. Sage Vishwamitra would accept nothing less than the whole of his kingdom, his palace and all his property.

"There is an alternative before you," he added. "You can swear that keeping your word is not your *dharma*. That would relieve you of your obligations."

But the king would not hear of such a thing. Ready to stand by his promise, he gave up his kingdom to the sage then and there. Vishwamitra stipulated that the king should make all arrangements for the performance of a *Rajasuya yagna*, and then leave the kingdom with his family and go into exile.

They returned to the palace, where the king formally handed over the reins of office, the throne, the palace and all the treasures in the royal coffers to Vishwamitra.

"You will take nothing with you," the sage insisted. "You, your wife and son will leave the kingdom with just the clothes you are wearing."

Bereft of all his wealth, bare of every ornament, the king prepared to leave the palace, accompanied by his queen and the young prince, his only son. As he was about to walk out of the gates of the palace, the sage came after him. "Stop," he commanded, "you cannot leave behind your debt to me. You had promised to make provisions for my first *rajasuya yagna*: that amount is still pending. Pay it up before you leave."

The King was astounded. He had given away everything he owned, and was absolutely penniless. How could he now make provisions for the elaborate *yagna*?

"Of course you have an option open to you: you can swear that *satya* (truth) is not important to you, and that will relieve you of this obligation."

"Never will I swerve from the way of Truth," said the king with conviction. "Only, I beg you, give me some time, and I will raise the funds required for the *yagna*."

And so it came to pass, that the king, his wife and son, travelled to the city of Kashi. Unable to find any employment, and constantly under pressure from Vishwamitra, the king was forced to sell his wife Chandramati as a domestic servant in the household of a *brahmin*; their son, Rohita, was also sold for a smaller sum of money to the same household, as a menial labourer. But the amount of money realised by this 'sale' was not enough to satisfy Vishwamitra. Finally, Harishchandra was forced to sell himself to the local executioner-cum-cremation ground keeper, as an assistant. His job would be to assist with the executions, and collect fees from the people who came to cremate their dead. The money acquired from the *brahmin* and the executioner was handed over to Vishwamitra for the *yagna*, and Harishchandra was freed from his 'debts' to the sage.

What followed was a period of harrowing misery for the erstwhile royal family. The queen toiled as a maidservant in the *brahmin*'s household; the prince was a child labourer to the family; and as for the king, his appearance became harsh and repulsive; his clothes were tattered and torn; the fumes from the funeral pyres clung to him, and he looked crude and awful.

One night, as he was standing guard at the gates of the cremation ground, he saw a weeping woman approach the gates with a child in her arms. She informed him that she had lost her young son and wanted to arrange for his cremation, as there was nobody else to help her.

"I will help you with the final rites, lady," Harishchandra said to her. "But first of all, you must pay me the fee for the cremation."

"Alas, I do not even have a copper coin to give you," wept the poor woman. "I have been sold as a slave and I do not even receive wages."

"The money I demand of you is not for my personal use," Harishchandra explained to her. "Part of the money goes to the executioner, my master; the other part goes to the local governor, for the upkeep of the cremation ground. I cannot let you enter this place without the payment of the required fee; that would be failing in my duty."

"What can I do?' wailed the bereft woman. "In the Name of God, show me some pity! Let me perform the last rites of this unfortunate son of mine."

"Then I suggest that you return to your master, and appeal to his compassion," suggested Harishchandra. "Ask him just for the amount to pay the cremation fee, and I will take care of the rest. Leave the body of your child with me, and I shall guard it till you return."

The woman returned sometime later. Her master had been adamant: he would not spare even a penny for the cremation.

"Alas, alas, what has become of me," she lamented. "Who

would believe that Prince Rohita, son of the great King Harishchandra, cannot even have the right of a destitute's funeral?"

Harishchandra was devastated. He and his wife had failed to recognise each other in their mean apparel and changed appearances. It was his own son who had been brought to him for cremation, and leave alone having the luxury to grieve for his bereavement, he had to demand payment of the fees from his own wife; for he could not be untrue to his master and his duty.

Restraining his grief and tears, Harishchandra forced his wife to part with her golden *mangalsutra* – the only ornament she had retained, in secret, till now. Having paid the fees with the money, the erstwhile king and queen prepared to cremate the mortal remains of their only child.

As the funeral pyre was about to be lit, a light flooded the cremation ground. Indra and his *devas* appeared before the grieving couple; accompanying them were the sages Vashishta and Vishwamitra. They applauded the king for his honesty and integrity, especially his firm adherence to truth. They touched the body of the dead prince, and the boy came alive.

"O, great king, we salute you for the ordeals you have gone through in your firm commitment to Truth," the sages said to him. "You will be restored to all your former glory and power, and you will be deeply venerated by future generations for your *satya vadana*, and ever admired as the epitome of Truth."

Such was the integrity of King Harishchandra, who valued Truth above all else.

THE SECOND GATEWAY TO HEAVEN:

TRUTH

Satyaat nasti paro dharma . There is no religion higher than truth. This is the injunction laid upon us by the ancient scriptures of India. Such is the respect we accord to *satya,* that the motto of the Government of India, the inscription on the seal of the state and the national emblem records yet another great statement from the Vedas: *Satyameva jayate.* Truth alone triumphs.

May I share with you the beautiful original verse from the *Mundaka Upanishad*:

> *Satyameva jayate naanritam*
> *Satyena pantha vitato devayanah*
> *Yenaa kramantyarishayo hyaaptakaamaa*
> *Yatra tat satyasya paramam nidhaanam*

Meaning:

> Truth alone triumphs; not falsehood.
> Through truth the divine path is spread out by which
> The sages whose desires have been completely fulfilled,
> Reach to where is that Supreme treasure of Truth.

Mahatma Gandhi, the father of our nation, and a role model for the ideal leader and good human being, regarded Hinduism as the most tolerant, most non-exclusive, most non-dogmatic and free religion of the world, and valued it as "a religion that offered the greatest scope for individual self-expression". He even said, "What of substance is contained in any other religion is always to be found in Hinduism. And what is not contained in it is insubstantial or unnecessary."

For Gandhi, the logical equivalent or manifestation of God was to be found in Truth. Truth is God, he declared. Truth is Rama, Narayana, Ishwara, Khuda, Allah and God. He frequently quoted with fervour the Sanskrit proverb with which we began this chapter: *satyaat nasti paro dharma*, and regarded it as the very foundation of his value system. The pursuit of truth, the attempt to realise truth in one's thought and action, he said, is the substance of the religion of man. "Devotion to truth," he wrote, "is the sole justification for our existence." Little wonder then, that his autobiography was entitled: "The Story of My Experiments with Truth".

During the days of his pilgrimage across India to spread his new-found faith, Guru Nanak was confronted several times by followers of existing faiths and *panths* (sects) who tried to discredit him and undermine his teachings. The leader of one such sect, once challenged Nanak thus: "You talk of God as if you knew Him. Can you show us where he dwells? And can you tell us what is His name?"

Guru Nanak's answer was simple and straight from the heart: "He is the One abiding Reality in this ever-changing world. And His name is *sat* – he is the Truth of all Truths."

This, the fundamental belief of Sikhism, is enshrined in the opening invocation of the prayer at the Gurudwara:

Ek Onkaar... Satnaam...

This is the opening line of that immortal scripture, the *Japji Sahib*. It is also the *Mool Mantra* or the root belief of Sikhism. *God is Universal, His Name is Truth*. The rest of the *sloka* is actually an expansion of the profound truth contained in these words.

> *Ek onkaar Sat Naam*
> *kartaa purakh nirbh-a-o nirvair akaal moorat*
> *ajoonee saibhn gur parsaad jap*
> *Aad sach jugaad sach.*
> *hai bhee sach naanak hosee bhee sach.*

There is Only One God Truth is His Name He is the Creator, Protector, without Fear, without Enmity, The First Entity, Never born, Self-perpetuating; With the Guru's grace: Recite! True in the beginning, True Through the Ages, True even now and says Nanak, will be True in the future too.

Truth is the very first step that the seeker has to take on the path to salvation. Truth is dear to God, and dear to men of God. It is every Guru's dearly held wish that his disciples should always bear witness to the truth in their daily life, and that they should always refrain from falsehood.

Once upon a time, there lived a holy man, a saint of God, who was in the habit of moving about from place to place, village to village, province to province, teaching everyone the good word of the Lord. He was a simple soul who lived a simple life; his needs were few, and all his ambitions were for the world beyond this one. He had a devoted disciple who went with him wherever he travelled, and was content to listen to the Guru's discourses, absorb the teachings into his mind and heart and serve him in whatever way he could. The Guru was an inspired speaker and a revered preceptor. Devout men were happy to offer him hospitality wherever he went. The Guru never expected much of them; a shelter for the night, and two simple meals a day for him and his disciple.

The guru and disciple had visited a village for a few days, accepting the hospitality of a local farmer. A stranger who came to listen to his discourse in the village, was so impressed by the guru's teachings, that he begged the holy man's permission to accompany him for a few days. "Your wisdom and your piety have influenced me so positively, that I long to be in your sacred company for a few more days," the stranger said to him.

"You can see that my *shishya* and I live the life of wandering ascetics," said the guru. "We live on the food given to us in charity by the villagers. It is by no means a life of comfort. However, if your thirst for truth is such that you can rise above such inconveniences, you are free to join us."

After a few days in the village, the guru took leave of the people, and set out for his next destination – a distant settlement which lay beyond a forest, located close to the village. His kind hosts packed ten *paranthas* for the travellers.

"There are three of you; the way through the forest is difficult and long, and so we have packed extra food for you," they said, as they took leave of the trio.

They set out early in the morning, and after several hours of strenuous walking, reached a clearance in the forest, where they sat down to rest and have a meal. When the packed food was opened, it was discovered that there were only nine *paranthas*. The Guru was astonished. "I know I haven't eaten anything since morning," he said; "so which one of you has eaten the *parantha?*" he asked the two younger men.

The disciple swore that he had not so much as laid hands on the food packet. "How can you even ask me such a question?" the newcomer shot back. "I have left behind all my worldly aspirations to walk the *gnana marga* with you. How could I even touch the food without your permission?"

The Guru was deeply disturbed. One of them was obviously lying. But who was the liar? Without raising any further questions, he signalled to the others to eat, and they set off through the forest, after a short rest.

Hardly had they walked for a mile or two, when they heard a fierce roar, and saw a ferocious lion standing across their path, ready to attack them. "Stand still," whispered the guru to the men. "Utter the name of the Lord in your heart, and pray to Him for your protection." Almost paralysed with fear, the men did as they were told. For what seemed to be a lifetime, the lion stared at them, as they prayed with all their might, their hearts beating fast. Then, the lion simply turned his back on them and walked away, as if he had lost all interest in them.

When the lion finally disappeared from sight, the two men fell at the Guru's feet. "It was your grace which protected us," they said, with deep gratitude. "How can we ever repay our debt to you? We are alive only because of you."

"That is as may be," said the guru. "But at least now, will you tell me which one of you ate that *parantha*?"

His disciple began to weep bitter tears. "O, Master, what an unfortunate being I am, that after so many years of following you faithfully, I am unable to inspire trust in you! Have I not listened to you speak of the power of truth day after day? Do I not know that there is no room in God's house for falsehood and lies? How could you be so unkind as to imagine that I would ever utter a lie to your face?"

As for the stranger, he retorted angrily, "I did not come with you for the sake of a few crumbs of food. I am surprised and shocked that a holy man like you should constantly dwell on such unworthy suspicions. Once and for all, I did not eat that *parantha*."

"Alright then," said the guru. "Let us move on."

As evening fell, our weary travellers were suddenly caught in a raging forest fire. Without the least warning, they found themselves trapped in a flaming circle which surrounded them and seemed to engulf them. Aloud, the guru uttered a prayer of appeal to the Lord, and implored the Almighty to come to their rescue. To the utter amazement of the two men, the fire seemed to recede as quickly as it had begun!

Exhausted, they sank to rest beneath a huge tree. The two young men were still panting with fear. As for the guru, he said to them sternly, "We have just passed through a life-threatening experience. I hope you will not continue to lie to me at such a time as this. Which one of you ate the *parantha*?"

"I wish I had been killed in the fire!" wept the disheartened disciple. "If there is one thing I have learnt at your feet, Master, it is never to utter a lie. You have been my father, mother, mentor and guide. How could I ever go against your precepts?"

"I repeat my question to you," said the guru to the newcomer. "Speak the truth. Did you eat that *parantha*?"

"I am actually beginning to lose my respect for you," said the man angrily. "Here I am, eager to pursue the higher truths, and you, my chosen teacher, continue to harp on that *parantha*! I tell you, I did NOT eat it."

Abruptly, the guru turned to his disciple and said to him, "Please dig the ground under that bush which you see at your feet."

Without asking any questions, the disciple wiped his tears and began to dig the earth under the bush. Hardly had he started digging, when he came across ten golden coins. He deposited the coins at the feet of the guru.

"Ten gold coins, and there are three of us here," said the guru. "We can take three coins each…"

"What of the tenth?" enquired the newcomer eagerly.

"That extra coin is reserved for the hungry soul who had to eat the tenth *parantha*," the guru replied, solemnly.

In an instant, the newcomer fell at the guru's feet. "Master, forgive me for lying to you. It was indeed I who stole the *parantha* and ate it when both of you were busy chanting your morning prayers. You, of course, are a man of God, and you will be true to your word, won't you? I get the fourth coin, right?"

I narrate this unfinished story only to illustrate to you, the 'convenience' of uttering truth and falsehood as it suits us! What we do not realise is that one falsehood leads on to another; to 'cover up' our earlier lies, we are forced to utter more lies, thus getting entrapped in a vicious cycle of falsehood. Out of greed, out of personal avarice, out of a desire to curry favour with those in office, we speak untruths: and let us not forget, exaggerated compliments, insincere statements, hypocritical utterances – all of them are equivalent to falsehood!

There is an incident from Gandhiji's childhood, narrated to us in his autobiography. Once, a British Inspector of Schools visited Gandhiji's school. Such visits were meant to check the proper functioning of the school and appraise the teaching-learning programme offered to the students. The Inspector decided to give a surprise spelling test to the children in Gandhiji's class. He read out five words from the English text and asked the children to write them down correctly. One of the words was 'kettle'; and Gandhiji misspelt the word. The teacher, who saw the mistake, whispered to Gandhiji to copy the correct spelling from the slate of the boy sitting next to him; Gandhiji understood what was happening; but he could not bring himself to copy from another. He retained the wrong spelling, and was pulled up by the inspector, as he was the only boy who had got the word wrong! To Gandhi, truth was more valuable than silver or gold!

It is said that when Alexander the Great came to India, two things impressed him most of all – the purity of the women of India, and the reverence for truth among all Indians. Therefore, he called this land *Indu*, meaning pure. I recalled this legend with regret, when a news headline caught my eye:

India was among the top ten nations of the world – in corruption and bribery! I shudder to think what Alexander would have said about our land, if he came to India now!

Satyam is described as one of the cardinal qualities of divine heritage or *daivi sampadi* in Chapter XVI of the Bhagavad Gita. Undoubtedly we will face great difficulties in our quest for Truth; but the man of divine qualities overcomes them by his perseverance on the path. Many of us, alas, give up the effort. "It is an impossible ideal to put into practice," we assert. "It is not just unattainable, it is impractical" we lament.

There are many excuses people offer for not adhering to the truth: we are afraid that the truth will hurt us and our chances of advancement and success; we use untruth as an excuse to cover up our deficiencies. It is only a man of courage who can stand up to the test of truth at all times in his life. Such is the value of truth that attainment to the Supreme Soul, the Almighty, is referred to as *sat-chit-ananda* or true, eternal bliss of awareness. We also have the much revered concept of *Satyam, Shivam, Sundaram* – the embodiment of truth, goodness and beauty, that is Lord Shiva. Further, the ten *yamas* or restraints recommended by the ancient scriptures, urge the seeker to refrain from falsehood.

Such is the power of the spoken word, that the Vedas urge us not merely to speak the truth, but also to speak only that truth which is pleasant, useful and cannot cause hurt to others.

Let me share with you one of those lesser known stories from the *Mahabharata*. At the end of the Kurukshetra war, Ashwatthama had vowed to destroy all the Pandava brothers before the dawn of the following day. Now, Ashwatthama was not only a great warrior and the son of Guru Dronacharya, but he was also a devout and pious *brahmin*, who had attained to the knowledge of the *Brahma Asthra* and the *Rudhra Asthra* – two of the most deadly and unassailable weapons. Sri Krishna knew that it would be difficult to save the Pandavas from his wrath. So he took them to the *ashram* of sage Durvasa and explained their predicament to the sage. He requested the sage to hide them in a cellar of the *ashram*, and not reveal their presence to Ashwatthama, if the latter came to look for them.

As we all know, Sage Durvasa had a great reputation for two things – his hot temper, and his adherence to the truth. But he also had great regard for Sri Krishna, and took pity on the Pandavas. He put them in the cellar, and promised to protect them. But to Sri Krishna, he said, "I am bound to obey your wishes, Lord. But do not expect me to utter a falsehood for any reason. If someone should come to me and enquire of their whereabouts, you know I must speak the truth."

"Not for anything in the world will I expect you to break your allegiance to truth or to utter a falsehood, O noble sage," Sri Krishna reassured him. "Speak the truth, by all means. But speak it in such a way, that no harm might come to those who have sought refuge under your care. After all, you have also given them your word that you will protect them."

As it happened, Ashwatthama arrived at Durvasa's *ashram* soon enough. The sage was seated in deep meditation on a straw mat; what the visitor did not know was that the mat was spread on top of that very trapdoor that led to the cellar, where the Pandavas had been hidden.

Ashwatthama, in his dire rage, rattled his sword and shouted curses on the Pandavas, disturbing the sage in his meditation. Durvasa opened his eyes, and rolled them in anger. " I am sorry to disturb you in your austerities," Ashwatthama said to him, "but you must tell me, in the name of truth, where the Pandavas are!"

"The Pandavas? The Pandavas? You come to ask me about the Pandavas in the midst of my daily *sadhanas*? Let me say to you, O foolish *brahmin*, those Pandavas are *beneath* me!"

Subdued, Ashwatthama hastily withdrew from the *ashram*, lest Durvasa should pronounce a curse on him. Truth had not been compromised; but the Pandavas who were literally 'beneath' the sage, were saved!

There is a beautiful incident narrated to us in the Gospels of Sri Ramakrishna. Sri Ramakrishna once said, "The virtue of truthfulness is most important. If a man always speaks truth and tenaciously holds to truth he will realise God; for God is

Truth. I prayed to the Divine Mother saying: 'Mother, here is knowledge, here is ignorance – take them both and give me pure love for You. Here is purity, here is impurity – take them both and give me pure love for You. Here is good, here is evil – take them both and give me pure love for You.' But I could not say, 'Here is truth, here is untruth.' For if I give up truthfulness in this way," said the Master, "how can I keep the truth that I have offered everything to the Mother of the universe?"

In his early days as the Messenger of Allah, Prophet Mohammed faced the enmity and hostility of certain powerful men. Chief among his enemies were the powerful leaders of the Koreishi tribe who spread slanders against him and incited people to stone him and attack him wherever he went.

The Prophet's uncle Abu Talib, an old man, was alarmed by the antagonism and hatred that his nephew had to face. In his anxiety and fear, he said to the Prophet, "My dear nephew, the Koreishites are strong and powerful – and they hate you! Heed my words: fear their power; do not provoke their wrath. Give up your preaching and return to your trade, I entreat you!"

Prophet Muhammed was unafraid. To the old uncle whom he loved and respected, Muhammed said gently but firmly, "Be not afraid for me! God will help me to stand by the truth – or give me death!"

Whenever Gurudev Sadhu Vaswani narrated this story to us, he would exclaim, "Truth, though she lead me to the gallows! Truth, though she take me through the fire!"

The path of Truth is not for the weak-willed and cowardly: as Emerson once put it, "God offers to every mind its choice between truth and repose. Take which you please – you can never have both".

To travel the path of truth is not only difficult, it needs a tremendous amount of discipline, courage, steadfastness and determination. But the rewards of following this path are spectacular and most important, eternal.

How may we follow the practice of truth in everyday life? Let me offer a few practical suggestions:

1. Become aware of why you do not speak the truth: is it out of fear? Or is it due to desire for gain? Or perhaps, out of ill-will and the wish to hurt others? Address the root cause, and do not let negative emotions like fear and greed and ill-will dictate your attitude. When you conquer these negative emotions, you learn to speak the truth in utter freedom.
2. Realise that the duty to speak the truth should not become a license to hurt another: therefore, practise truth along with kindness.
3. Speak the truth at the appropriate time: helpful suggestions and honest utterances should not be uttered when your listeners are not prepared to take them.

4. Do not rehearse half-truths or lies as excuses to utter to friends: if there has been a lapse on your part, admit the truth.

5. Learn the art of sincere apology. Learning to say sorry is one of the most difficult acts of truth. It involves being honest about yourself and being honest to the other person as well.

6. Not just outright lies, but also exaggerations and omissions amount to falsehood: therefore, in all important matters, learn to speak the truth, the whole truth and nothing but the truth.

7. Remember that gossip, slander and rumour are some of the worst forms of falsehood. Refrain from these at all times, and at all costs.

8. Hypocrisy and pretence are also akin to falsehood. Be aware of who you are and what your limitations are. Do not pretend to be what you are not.

9. Practise honesty in all your transactions, especially when they relate to money matters. Avoid malpractices in all business dealings.

10. Offering or accepting a bribe is also a form of dishonesty. Refrain from corrupting others; equally, do not seek illicit gains for yourself by accepting bribes.

11. To follow the path of truth – live a simple life.

••••••••

Humility does not consist in hiding our talents and virtues, or in thinking of ourselves as being worse than we really are; but in realising that all that we are, and all that we have, are freely given to us by God.

J.P. Vaswani

••••••••

The Greatest Among The Gods

Once Rishi Brighu was overwhelmed by the desire to find out who, among the Holy Trinity of Brahma, Shiva and Vishnu, should be worshipped as the greatest. The sage decided that *He* would be the greatest, who showed the greatest degree of egolessness, forbearance and forgiveness.

At first, Brighu made his way to the abode of Lord Brahma. Having arrived in the presence of the Lord, Brighu simply ignored Him, not touching His feet or bowing before Him, refusing even to acknowledge His presence. Lord Brahma was incensed. He rose to pronounce a terrible curse on the sage. However, He was restrained by His Divine Consort Saraswati who said to Him, "Dear Lord, please bear with Brighu this once. There must be some reason for his strange behaviour."

Lord Brahma relented, and sage Brighu made a safe escape.

His next stop was at Mount Kailash, the abode of Lord Shiva. Approaching the Lord who sat in divine meditation, Brighu began a tirade. "Look at you!" he laughed scornfully. "Your body is smeared with ashes and You are garlanded by snakes! You must be mad!"

Lord Shiva would have hurled His *trishul* at Brighu in divine wrath, had not Mother Parvati held him back, saying, "Let him go, my Lord, just this once!"

Fleeing for his life from Kailash, he went to Vaikunth, where Lord Vishnu, the Great Preserver of the Universe lay in his Divine *yoganidra*. Emboldened by the peaceful sleep of the Lord, Brighu did what was unimaginable – he kicked the Lord in the chest, and shouted, "How can You go off to sleep, without a care for Your task of sustaining life in this world?"

The moment He opened His eyes, Lord Vishnu clutched the feet of the sage. "Forgive me O Holy one!" He pleaded. "Your holy, sacred foot must surely have been hurt by the hardness of my chest! How can I soothe the pain that I have inadvertently caused to you – one of My greatest devotees?"

Brighu fell in tears at the Lord's feet. "O lord! Forgive my arrogance and folly, for I set out to judge You! O Lord of Supreme Compassion, how will I ever wash away the terrible sin of having kicked Your holy chest? What a great shame and disrepute will come on my head!"

"How can any father be angry with the infant who kicks his chest?" said the Lord, smiling. "You are My loving son, and you have taken a child's liberty with your Father. Your foot print shall remain imprinted on my chest, for ages to come."

4

THE THIRD GATEWAY TO HEAVEN : HUMILITY

Many years ago, my Beloved Gurudeva Sadhu Vaswani told us the story of a seeker of God. In quest of the heaven-world, he moves, from place to place, and, after much weary wandering, finds himself standing at the gate of the heaven-world.

The gate-keeper asks him, "Who are you?"

And the seeker answers, "I am a scholar and a teacher."

"Wait here a while," says the gate-keeper, "I shall go in and report your arrival."

Soon, the gate-keeper returns with the answer, "I cannot let you in, for the Master says there is no place for teachers in the heaven-world."

I hope my teacher-friends are not upset by the course this story is taking: This story is about a teacher who had not yet found his true vocation. As Gurudev Sadhu Vaswani used to tell us, "So many teachers, are vain. They parade their little learning. How can there be a place in the heaven-world for those who live in a world of pride and vanity?" But let us return to the story.

Disappointed, the seeker is about to turn away, when he hears the words, "O teacher! The dust of dead words clings to thee! Wash thyself of this dust in the waters of silence!"

The teacher follows the advice given to him. Everyday he sits in silence and listens to the words of the saints and sages. Gradually, his 'self–consciousness' drops; he becomes humble. And one day, as he sits in meditation with a true longing in his heart for the Lotus-feet of the Lord, he hears the words:

"Blessed is the life of a helper and a servant! If you would enter the heaven-world, breathe out this aspiration that you may be a servant of all, a servant of teachers and pupils, of the lonely and lowly ones, of all men and birds and animals, a servant of God and His creation!"

The seeker breathes out this aspiration, again and again. And, all of a sudden, he finds himself back at the portals of heaven. This time, the gates of heaven are wide open. The angels are

> **Pride says to itself, "My will be done." Humility says to God, "Thy will be done."**
> *- Kent Crockett.*

there to greet him, saying, "Blessed indeed are you, O servant of God and His suffering creation! Enter in and behold the Master's face – pure and fair, beyond compare!"

Yes, the Kingdom of God, the *ashram* of the Guru, the path of discipleship is for the humble at heart. Unfortunately, many of us are proud, vain and lost in ego! When we are lost in ego, we become blind to wisdom, and can only wander from darkness to deeper darkness!

> **Humility is the key to God's heart that unlocks His mercy.**
> *- Kent Crockett*

When I took leave of my near and dear ones and sought refuge at Gurudev Sadhu Vaswani's feet, the very first lesson he taught me was the lesson of humility.

"The God that rules millions is the ego," he said. "Enthrone God in your heart – the God of love – if you wish to cease wandering!"

When I asked him how I could enthrone in my heart the God of love, his answer was simple: "Be humble as ashes and dust!"

The truly humble are the truly happy. And what we need to be truly happy, is not a change in outer circumstances, but deliverance from slavery to the self, the petty ego. This petty ego sits as a tyrant on some of us, robbing us of the bliss that is our birthright: i.e. heritage as children of God. For God built this world in beauty, and we were meant to live our lives in the fullness of freedom and joy. Man was meant to live like a song-bird, unfettered, free. Alas, man finds himself cribbed, cabined, confined. He has become like a bird in a cage – he is trapped in the cage of self-centeredness!

Not until self-centeredness goes may man become truly happy and free: and the prison of self-centeredness opens with the key of humility. Especially important for the seeker on the path is humility: for it sets free the swan bird of the soul, and the soul can soar into radiance and joy!

Let me quote to you the beautiful lines of Sant Kabir:

> *Mitha bolan, nih chalan*
> *Hathau bhi kuchch de,*
> *Rab tinaa de paas,*
> *Vo jhangal kiyun dhundhe.*

In translation, this beautiful verse means:

> Speak sweetly,
> Walk humbly,
> Let your hands never be tired of giving.
> Then why need you to the forest go,
> The Lord is with you already!

If you do these things dutifully, then there is no need for you to go to a forest and meditate. There is no need for you to go in quest of God. For God, the Source of Joy and Happiness will come in quest of you – and meet you.

A veritable roadmap for the 'Life Beautiful' is given us in those three injunctions: (1) Speak sweetly; (2) Walk humbly and (3) Let your hands never be tired of giving.

When I put this across to one of my friends, he said to me, a little apologetically, "With all due respect to you Dada, if we walk humbly and talk gently in that big bad world out there, people will walk all over us! I am afraid, that in today's harsh environment, humility and gentleness are apt to be taken as signs of weakness, rather than goodness!"

I said to him, "I beg to differ with that view. On the contrary, I feel very strongly that there is an indefinable sense of dignity about every truly humble person."

The great saint, Sri Ramkrishna Paramhansa, used to tell his disciples, to deliberate on the mantra: *Na Hum! Na Hum! Tu ho! Tu ho!* I am nothing – Thou Alone art! Thou art the Creator of this Universe. Me? I am nothing. When you realise your insignificance, you will automatically become humble.

Guru Arjun Dev, in *Sri Sukhmani Sahib*, says, 'The true *Brahmagyani* is one who lives in humility.' A true *Brahmagyani* is pure as a lily and humble as ashes and dust. He immerses himself in austerity and lives a life of simplicity.

It is said of Leo Tolstoy, the great Russian writer, that when he realised the truth of his being, he renounced his vast material wealth, high social status and power. He went and lived among the poor peasants of Russia.

Think of Sri Krishna, the Lord of the Universe. He humbled Himself to become the charioteer of His dear, devoted disciple, Arjuna. Maha Vishnu became *Partha Sarathi* to demonstrate to us His *saushilya* – the quality of gentle, loving kindness – that we must all emulate.

Mahatma Gandhi's poverty and austere life style is a legend of our times. Clad in his loincloth an *angavastra*, he conquered a million hearts, the might of the British Empire bowed before him.

In India, we have the beautiful tradition of greeting everyone we meet with folded hands and the reverential greeting: *Namaste!* It is a beautiful gesture of respect for the other person, and a spontaneous act of humility that ennobles both him who salutes and him who receives the salutation. It is ridiculous to think that we 'lower' our dignity in any way by saluting another thus: we would do well to remember that it is the God within the human form that we salute thus.

Why should we be humble in our dealings with others? Because Lord Krishna resides within everyone of us. He is omnipotent, omnipresent, omniscient. Lord Krishna's beauty, art, intellect, knowledge and ability are supreme. We are like a speck of dust, insignificant before His power and magnificence. And yet, He comes to live in the humble abode of our heart. Should this not teach us to be humble? If Lord Krishna Himself resides in the people we meet, how can we presume to be haughty and proud before Him? Should we not be soft, gentle, reverential and sweet to the Lord?

Another thing necessary for all of us, is humility of the heart. Be humble; be humble as a blade of grass. Once Gurudev Sadhu Vaswani was asked: What kind of persons would you like to associate with? Rich and famous, intelligent and scholarly, elite and sophisticated, or beautiful and charming? Gurudev Sadhu Vaswani with a magical smile replied, "My heart moves out to those who are humble. For the humble are pure at heart. They are the loved ones." Therefore let us learn to be humble and earn the grace of God.

King James the Second was a powerful monarch of England. Once, some of his important papers went missing. He searched for them high and low, but could not find them. Calling his personal attendant, he asked him if he had seen the papers. The personal attendant replied, "Your Majesty, I do not know any thing about the 'papers'. I have not seen them at all!" Hearing this, the king flew into a rage. He slapped the attendant hard, and said, "You always give me the same answer whenever you misplace something."

The poor attendant was abashed. He bowed low before the king and said, "My Lord, please forgive me." The servant was in no way responsible for the loss of the papers. But he knew that the king had the authority to punish him.

Three days later, the king's minister brought some documents for the king's perusal. The king opened the file and was surprised to find those needed papers inside. The king recalled that he had sent these very documents to his minister with the instruction, to read them carefully and make a gist of the same, for his perusal. The king also recalled how furious he had been with his personal attendant for apparently misplacing the documents. Immediately, he called his attendant and in the very presence of his minister, the king asked the attendant for forgiveness.

The attendant was taken aback. "Your Majesty," he exclaimed, "you are the monarch of this country. I am but a humble servant. Who am I to forgive you?"

"No, no," the king insisted, "unless you forgive me for my harsh behaviour, God will not pardon me. You were innocent. Even if you had made the mistake, I had no right to slap you." The King somehow convinced the attendant to say, 'Your Majesty, I forgive you.'

James II, was truly a noble King. He practised humility in daily life.

Once I visited a family. The *dhobi* (washerman) had brought in clothes and was meekly standing in a corner. Near by was an empty chair. I said to the *dhobi*, "Why don't you sit down on that chair." Hearing this, the head of the household felt disturbed. He said to me, "We must keep them in their place. By showing them undue kindness, we will only spoil them." Such is our false ego and pride.

We are told that Philip II (the father of Alexander the Great) employed two men whose sole responsibility was to address him twice each day. Their morning duty? To say: "Philip, remember that you are but a man." And in the evening? To ask: "Philip, have you remembered that you are but a man?"

Many great men of the modern world were men of simplicity and humility. Indeed their humility served to set them apart and added to their greatness.

Michael Faraday, the great scientist was a simple soul. His simple clothes and modest behaviour often concealed from others his superior intelligence and genius.

Once, a government official wished to meet Faraday. He went to the Royal Society where Faraday often worked, and asked to see the great scientist. He was directed to the lab where Faraday used to conduct his experiments.

When the visitor entered the lab, he found it empty except for an old man in an overall who was washing bottles at a sink.

"Excuse me, are you an employee of the Royal Society?" the visitor asked him.

"Yes, I have served the Society for over four score years," said the old man. "What can I do for you?"

"Are you happy with wages you get here?" the visitor persisted.

"I am content," smiled the old man.

"What's your name, by the way?"

"They call me Michael Faraday," came the reply.

The visitor was mortified. He had mistaken the great scientist for a security guard. How could a great man be so simple, he wondered. Or, was he great *because* he was utterly simple?

Gandhiji too, surprised people by his simplicity and humility. One day, Richard Cregg, an American admirer of Gandhiji, arrived at the Sabarmati *Ashram* to meet the Mahatma. He was told that Gandhiji was in the common dining hall.

Cregg wondered if Gandhiji was having a meal and whether he would disturb him by calling on him then.

However, he found the Dining Hall and entered inside only to find the great-souled leader seated on the ground, peeling vegetables for the morning meal.

"Come in, come in," Gandhiji greeted the visitor cheerfully. "I'm sorry you find me occupied with my duty at the *ashram*, but I'm delighted to meet you! Welcome to Sabarmati *Ashram*!"

The American was overwhelmed by Gandhiji's utter simplicity. In a trice, he was sitting next to Gandhiji, helping him with the vegetables!

Of what are we proud, I often ask myself. Power, wealth, fame, youth, beauty — all, all are transient. As great ones have continually demonstrated, even world conquerors leave this earth empty-handed. Sant Dadu Dayal tells us:

> When one lost what was one's own, and abandoned all pride of birth: when vain-glory has dropped away, then, only then, is one face to face with the Creator.

Of the great Emperor Shah Jahan, we are told, that during a hot summer night, as he was resting in his private apartments, he was suddenly overcome by thirst. He clapped his hands, as was his wont, to call a servant to attend to him – but it so happened that none of the palace servants happened to be nearby.

The emperor arose from his royal couch and went to the pitcher of water which was always kept near his bed. The silver jug was absolutely empty!

By now, the emperor was parched with thirst. He went out into the enclosed courtyard which adjoined his private chamber, for he knew there was a well there, from which he could draw water. As he was unused to this task, he hurt himself badly on the crank of the pulley, when he tried to haul the container of water towards himself. The pain in his hand was quite sudden and severe, and he actually cried out in agony. At that moment, the thought flashed across his mind that here he was, an emperor – but he was so inept that he could not even draw water from the well to slake his own thirst! O Beloved Lord!" he exclaimed, "I thank you for this experience. How foolish and clumsy I am – and yet, in Thy inscrutable grace, Thou hast made me an emperor!"

It was the great Sufi saint Rumi, who said: "When thou thyself shall come to be, then the beloved Lord will thou find. Therefore, O wise man, try to lose thyself, and feel humility." He adds, for further emphasis, "Egoism and self-will are opposed to the Holy Name; the two cannot dwell in the same house. None can serve the Lord without humility; the self-willed mind is worthless."

Guru Gobind Singh tells us:

> Emperors before whom strong armed kings did meekly bow their heads in countless numbers:
> Who possessed great elephants with golden trappings, proud and painted with brilliant colours:

Millions of horses swifter than the wind which bounded o'er
the world:
What mattered it how mighty were these emperors?
All at the last went hence
With nothing, bare of foot.

We read an amusing anecdote about St. Peter who once stood at the Pearly Gates of Heaven, reading the judgements that admitted the Blessed Souls to God's presence.

To a rich philanthropist who had spent much of his wealth on feeding the poor, he said, "I was hungry, and you gave me to eat. So enter the kingdom of the Lord."

To a man of service who had dug canals and wells, and installed hand-pumps in remote draught-prone villages, he said, "I was thirsty, and you gave me to drink. So come in."

In the line stood a poor clown who had worked in a circus and made people laugh. He trembled as he stepped before the gates of Heaven. With bowed head he waited for St. Peter's judgement. St. Peter smiled and said to him, "I was sad and depressed, and you made me laugh. Enter the kingdom of Heaven."

Graciousness and humility are instinctive to great people. In fact their personalities are only further enhanced – even adorned – by this special quality.

At a grand banquet where President and Mrs. Roosevelt were present, an old man approached Mrs. Roosevelt and greeted her respectfully. She returned the greeting graciously and spoke to him for some time.

Emboldened by her courteous behaviour, the old man said to her, "Madame, may I bring my wife to you – she thinks the world of you – and she will be delighted to have the opportunity to meet you in person!"

"May I ask you how old your wife is, Sir?"

"She is about eighty-two, ma'am," the old man replied. "She is seated just outside this hall, in the anteroom. Shall I bring her here to meet you?"

"No, Sir," smiled Mrs. Roosevelt. "I should go and see her. You see, I'm fifteen years younger than your wife, and I should go to see her – not the other way round!"

Truly, Mrs. Roosevelt was adorned by her humility!

When the distinguished scientist, Sir Isaac Newton lay on his deathbed, a friend said to him, "It must be a source of great pride and gratification to you to know that you have managed to penetrate to the depth of nature's wonderful laws!"

"Far from feeling proud," Newton said to him, "I feel like a little child who has found a few bright coloured shells and pebbles, while the vast ocean of truth stretches unknown and unexplored before me!"

All men of true learning are truly humble!

It was John Ruskin who said, "The first test of a truly great man is his humility."

The great Chinese philosopher, Confucius, also tells us that humility is the solid foundation of all virtues.

Our ancient Indian sages and poets also admired humility as the greatest virtue in man. To illustrate this they compared a great man with a bountiful tree laden with fruit, which bows down with its load of fresh fruits.

Rahman was a famous Muslim poet who wrote lovely lyrics expressing *Prem Bhakti*. He also happened to be a very rich man who spent his great wealth not on his own personal luxuries, but for the benefit of the poor and needy.

While he gave away alms to *sadhus* and *fakirs*, he always bowed his head low, and refused to look at them.

Noticing this, a friend asked him, "Why do you bow down your head while giving alms to the poor?"

"They praise me for my humble mite… which in reality is that of the Almighty," replied Rahman. "I am only His agent, the instrument of His divine plan. Therefore I bow down my head in embarrassment, for I do not deserve their praise and thanks!"

The friend became speechless with admiration for Rahman's humility.

Thou shalt seek the lowest place! I wonder how many of you will abide by this commandment in this day and age when there is a scramble for power and greatness. Everyone is seeking the highest place! Governments are toppled; board rooms have become battlegrounds; sons oust their fathers; coups are staged; fierce rivalry and competition prevail. Everyone wants greatness!

But the true student of the Gita, the devotee of the Gita, will always seek the lowest place. This has been the witness of the great ones of humanity – and Sri Krishna Himself demonstrates this wonderful ideal to us, by His own personal example.

Think of Jesus Christ. At the Last Supper, on the eve of His crucifixion, in the very last hours of His earth pilgrimage, He picks up a bowl of water and a towel, and He washes and wipes the feet of His own disciples. He also tells them words which we would do very well to heed: "He that would be the greatest among you, let him be a servant of all."

This is the witness of the great ones — they seek the lowest place.

> He that is down need fear no fall
> He that is low no pride:
> He that is humble ever shall
> Have God to be his guide.

These are the words of John Bunyan in his book, *Pilgrim's Progress*.

Think of Gurudev Sadhu Vaswani. One day some of us were sitting in a group, allotting duties for the *Janmashtami langar* which was to be held a few days later. Gurudev Sadhu Vaswani saw us and enquired as to what we were discussing.

"We are allotting duties to each one for the *langar*, Dada," we said to him.

"What duty are you giving me?" he enquired of us.

One of us said to him, "Dada, it will be wonderful if you could join us during the *langar*. Your 'duty' would be to remain seated at the entrance to the hall where *langar* is held – and to bless each one who enters to take his or her place in the hall. That would really make our day!"

"No," said the Master. "I will take a different duty. I shall sweep the floor after each batch has eaten, to get the hall clean and ready to receive the next batch." Gurudev Sadhu Vaswani always sought the lowest place!

The Gita tells us to walk the little way, to walk the way of humility. This is the way on which the grace of God will be poured upon us abundantly! God's grace is like holy water – and water, as you all know, seeks the lowest place. If you have occupied the lowest place, the grace of God will flood into your life, and you will not only be truly blessed, but you will also be a source of blessing to many!

Holy men and sages tell us that humility is the true mark of the evolving soul. You maybe assured that it is not easy to attain – for it involves the utter effacement of the ego.

Alas, for many of us, I'm afraid, the ego is unconquerable. Man has conquered space; man has conquered the sky; man has controlled even the courses of rivers and the growth of the great forests – but man has not found it easy to control or conquer the ego.

It is the presence of unconscious *vasanas* (subtle desires) in the mind which give rise to ego. Most of our human interactions are based on the ego. In fact, for the vast majority of the people, their ego is their identity. When people are disgruntled or disappointed, ego begins to rise like high fever. They try to assert themselves, to assert their identity. Little do they realise that ego only blocks the flow of energy and power into their lives. When ego becomes the source of your motivation and initiative, you can achieve little; but when the ego is subdued, the Supreme Self becomes the source of your advancement and initiative. This is what makes the best human achievements possible!

Alas, for most of us in the modern age, complete relaxation of the ego is achieved only during the sleeping state! Ego is then set aside, *not* by a process of conscious effort, but by a biological, unconscious process. This is why we say, "He/she is sleeping peacefully as a child."

When you are able to set aside your ego by a conscious voluntary effort, through your own intuition and understanding, you have every reason to conquer yourself — for you have taken the first step on the path of liberation and enlightenment. Of such a man, Chaitanya Mahaprabhu says:

> One who is humbler
> Than a blade of grass
> And yet, more enduring than a tree:
> One who gives respect to those who lack it —
> Such a devotee is fit to sing
> The praises of the Lord at all times!

Many distinguished scientists have said that when man realises the vastness, the grandeur and the immensity of the universe we live in, and our own insignificance in the universal scheme of things, it is impossible for us to feel egotistical and proud.

Just think – at one time, the Universe existed; Time existed; but planet earth did not exist; the solar system did not exist; and, in course of time, a day will come when this earth will cease to exist; and the solar system would have disintegrated. And yet, Time will live on...

Someone asked Mahatma Gandhi, "Why are you called Mahatma, or great soul?" Gandhiji replied, "Because I consider myself the least of human beings." What he meant was that one had to take the lowest place possible, in order to become truly great in the eyes of God. Therefore Gandhiji always remained humble – always a student, always a servant of others.

Let me warn you too, against false humility or superficial humility. I am sorry to say that people often assume false humility for a particular purpose. Thus subordinates bow and scrape before their superiors. When you assume false humility for a selfish purpose, it is not really humility at all – but hypocrisy!

Even the greatest among us fall victims to the ego. The *Mahabharata* tells us the story of how the Pandavas were taught valuable lessons in humility, which made them better human beings.

Bhima learnt his lesson when Draupadi begged him to bring her a rare flower. She had been captivated by the fragrance of the flower, and wanted more like it. Eager to fulfil every wish of his beloved, Bhima set out to get the flower.

As he crossed the rocky paths and thick forests at breakneck speed, Bhima approached a grove, where a huge monkey lay across his path.

"Get out of my way," he snarled at the creature. "I'm in a hurry, so don't keep me waiting."

The monkey opened its eyes and looked at him sleepily. "I am too old and tired to move," it said to Bhima. "Why don't you just lift my tail and shift it to one side, so that you may pass me?"

Arrogantly, Bhima started to lift its tail with disdain, but to his utter shock and dismay, he could not even stir it! Gritting his teeth, summoning all his strength, he tried hard to push the tail away. He was now perspiring heavily, and his breath was gasping – but he could not budge the tail even an inch.

In an instant, Bhima realised that this was no ordinary old monkey, as he had assumed it to be. Filled with humility, he bowed down to the monkey and said, "Please reveal your true identity to me. I have learnt a valuable lesson from you today."

The 'old monkey' revealed himself to be none other than Hanuman, beloved of Sri Rama. He had come to meet Bhima, test his strength and bestow his blessings upon him. For both of them were sons of Vayu, the Wind-God. When Hanuman embraced him and blessed him, Bhima felt a fresh energy, a new spirit and immense strength flowing into his body – much stronger and humbler now than the inflated, egotistic personality which he had asserted a short while ago!

When the Kurukshetra war was over, Arjuna prepared to alight from his chariot. He was proud of his might and valour, which had been the chief factor in defeating Kauravas. How many *astras*, how many celestial weapons had been directed against him! But he had bravely stood his ground against them. They could not even touch him! Now it was time to leave the battleground, and rest his weary limbs.

Before he alighted, Arjuna said to Sri Krishna, "Please alight now, Lord. You must be tired too!"

"After you, Arjuna," said Sri Krishna with a smile. "I am your *Sarathi*. How can the driver alight before his passenger does? You must be the first to get off."

Delighted by the Lord's gracious reply, Arjuna descended from the chariot and prepared to hold the reins of the horses, so that Sri Krishna could alight. But to his surprise, Sri Krishna asked him to go away, and stand at a distance.

When Arjuna was at a safe distance, Sri Krishna alighted from the chariot. In a moment, the chariot was blown to pieces, disintegrating before their very eyes!

Arjuna realised that what had kept him alive and prevented his chariot from utter destruction was not his valour, but the Lord's presence. It was Sri Krishna's grace and power that had stopped all the celestial weapons hurled at Arjuna. If the Lord had alighted from the chariot first, Arjuna would have been blown to bits without his divine protection. This was why Sri Krishna had asked him to walk away before He Himself alighted from the chariot, thus making it defenceless and subject to the power of the various *astras* hurled against it!

Humility is not weakness: I regard it as a truly powerful weapon that can break the tyranny of the ego!

May I share with you a few simple suggestions in this regard?

1) When in the midst of friends or strangers, refrain from pushing yourself forward. Watch how at the slightest excuse there arises the tendency to show yourself off.

2) Refrain from too much talk. The less you talk, the less you will be noticed and the more you will be permitted to recede into the background.

   As it is, we tend to talk too much. Some of us constantly try to monopolise the conversation. Sometimes, friends come to us to unburden themselves – and instead of listening to them with understanding and sympathy, we overwhelm them with our discourse on endurance and patience. Oh how we love 'lecturing' to others! If only we could remain silent and let others talk, it would do us a world of good.

3) Always keep clear of the desire of telling others of your life and achievements, your inner struggles and experiences, your opinions and aspirations. Learn to live and grow in the thought that you are a tiny particle of dust – and that no one will miss you when you are away.

4) Remember – your real value lies not in your outer, empirical self, but in your inner, imperishable Self; and this inner Self cares not for the applause of others. It is firmly established in itself.

5) Cultivate friendship with this inner Self. And meditate on the significant words of the Gita:

He who hath conquered
His lower self of cravings and desires,
He hath his Supreme Friend found
In the Self, immortal, true!
But he who still a victim is
To his appetites and passions,
Verily, the Self becometh to him,
Hostile as an enemy!

The ego is a thief; the ego is our most dangerous enemy; it is the force that separates the soul from God. It is the impenetrable wall which hides us from the Light with dark shadows of 'I', 'Me' and 'Mine' falling on us, obstructing our vision.

There is a phrase in the *Gurbani:* Ego is a disease. Ego is a disease worse than cancer. Its cells multiply themselves to ruin us. Fortunately, its cure is within us. The moment we look within, and see our true self, our ego falls off and disappears. That is why saints and sages teach us, 'Know thyself'. When you realise that you are not the physical body, but the soul within, your ego will vanish. For in that awareness, there is no place for ego.

Of what are we proud? Youth, beauty, wealth, power – all, all are transient. Sant Kabir sings:

> One enemy or the other
> Always treads upon your heels:
> Lust may be driven out, but anger lingers;
> And greed will stay when anger goes;
> And then, when greed is gone,
> Vain glory, vanity and the wish to be honoured
> Fills the emptiness left in the mind...

Only when all association with *aham* – 'I' ness – is dissolved through genuine humility, can enlightenment, illumination and union with the divine be achieved.

When the ego goes, the light of God glows.

· · · · · · · ·

True faith is the belief that
whatever may happen,
God loves me,
He is always there for me!

J. P. Vaswani

· · · · · · · ·

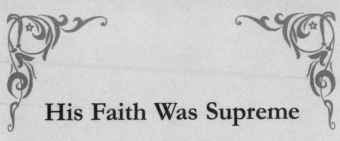

His Faith Was Supreme

The story of Prahlada is beloved of all devout Hindus, especially the children. Prahlada is the very symbol of absolute faith and unquestioning belief in the Lord.

He is tormented, ill-treated, tortured by his father Hiranya Kashipu, who expects all his people to worship *him* as God.

Prahlada refuses, "Father," he says, "Hari is real and Him I worship."

The annoyed king orders Prahlada to be flung amidst serpents. But they do not harm him – for he sees the Lord in them!

The king orders the boy to be trampled over by an elephant. But the elephant refuses to move – for Prahlada sees the Lord in the elephant!

He is thrown from a steep cliff. The earth receives him lovingly in her arms unharmed.

He is flung into the sea. The waves refuse to drown him. He sees the play of the Lord in the rise and fall of the waves.

He is thrown into a roaring fire. In the flames he beholds the face of the Lord – and of course the flames do not burn him!

"Where is thy Hari?" roars his infuriated father.

"I see Hari everywhere" replies the child. "He is behind me, before me, above me, around me. He is in the speck of dust. He is in this mighty pillar!"

In anger, Hiranya Kashipu strikes the pillar – and out of the pillar Sri Hari appears as Narsimha, to protect His beloved devotee Prahlada!

5

THE FOURTH GATEWAY TO HEAVEN: FAITH

If, like many people, you also cherish the fond belief that heaven is a place "up above there, somewhere", then, let me tell you, you need not give in to despair about the 'heights' to which you would be obliged to 'climb'; I believe God created us mortals with two very special wings – Faith and Hope.

Faith is the fourth Gateway to Heaven. Faith is not a behaviour pattern; nor an intellectual attribute; it is, like love and compassion, a matter of the heart.

I am reminded of the days of my youth, when railway journeys were slow and relaxed, and when the hectic rush for 'booking' and 'reservations' were unknown. People would amble into the Railway Station an hour or two before the journey and buy tickets at the 'window' (it was not even a counter then) and then sit back and wait for the train. With those tickets they could get into any compartment (of course, they would have to buy First class, Inter class, Second class or Third class tickets) and take the seat of their choice. Some made a beeline for the coveted corner seat; some occupied the upper berth for which there would be few takers. The point is, the ticket bought at the window was enough to assure them of the journey to their chosen destination.

Faith is just such a ticket to heaven, which you can count on. And the process of getting this ticket is still relatively uncomplicated, as in the early days. To continue the metaphor,

I might add: just leave it to God – I mean, entrust your life into His safe hands – and He will deliver the ticket of Faith to your heart!

> **Some one asked me: "What makes your life beautiful?"**
> **I said: "I have a friend."**
> **Yes, He protects me. He guards me in illness. He blesses me every day.**
> **And He stretches forth His Arms of Love to enfold me in silence and darkness of the night.**
> **He is your Friend, too. Indeed, He is the Friend of friends.**
> **And may your faith in Him shine and shine and make your crowded life truly divine!**
> **—*Sadhu Vaswani***

He who has faith, has everything. For, as the wonderful proverb tells us, faith can indeed move mountains. The Bible also tells us the same thing. *Everything is possible to him who believeth.*

Therefore, if you wish to grow in faith, then pray for faith as a famished person prays for food and a thirsty person for water. What is it to have faith? It is nothing but to accept God's plan for you—to surrender to the Will Divine. It is to feel sure that whatever God does is always for the best. It is to grow in the realisation that when God seems to deny you—His own child—something which you regard as good, He designs to give you something better!

Sri Ramakrishna, speaking to his disciples, said again and again, "The man of faith is like a python. He moves not in search of food, his food comes to him."

It was an enlightened singer of the spirit, who sang of God thus:

> O ye pilgrims on the path!
> Cast all thy cares upon the Lord
> And chant His Name
> By day and by night
> And fill the earth
> With the fragrance of Heaven!
> He, the Lord of love
> Doth in love become
> A burden bearer
> Of His bhaktas all!

What a beautiful conviction this — to rest in the belief that He will bear all our burdens! This conviction will not come to us by reading books or listening to lectures. It is not a matter of ratiocination or argumentation. It will not come by intellectual analysis or reasoning of the mind. It will come only by faith!

Faith belongs to those of us who have learnt to love. For in love, we renounce our little 'ego', and so rise above the cares and worries of earthly existence. In love we know that we belong to Him who takes care of us as a mother takes care of her only child. Such faith is not just reassuring and comforting: it brings about miracles in your daily life.

A pious lady was talking to her little nephew about the efficacy of prayer. Suddenly, the little boy asked, "If I ask God to help me find my marbles, will He answer my prayer?" The lady assured him that God would indeed do so.

"May I kneel down and pray to God now?" the boy asked.

His aunt having given her consent, the little boy knelt by his chair, closed his eyes and prayed silently. Then he rose, and went about his work contentedly.

Next day, the lady asked him if he had found his marbles. She hoped that his simple faith would not be tested adversely.

"No aunt, I haven't found them," the boy replied. "But God has made me not want to find them!"

God does not always answer our prayers in the way we wish or expect, but if we are sincere, He will take from us the desire for what is contrary to His Will!

Faith is not just a solution to all our problems – it is a transformation of our inner existence; it helps us cultivate hope and optimism, which have the power to change our attitude, change our pattern of thinking, and thus change our lives for the better!

There is a wonderful prayer ascribed to Plato; "Lord of Lords, grant me the good, even though I may not ask for it. And keep me away from evil, even though I ask for it!"

My Master, Sadhu Vaswani, often said to us, "God upsets our plans to set up His own. And His plans are always perfect. In His Divine Wisdom He knows what is not good for us, and He will not grant it to us."

Faith is not just simplistic fulfillment of all our material desires. Our prayers are not necessarily answered in the ways in which we expect them to be answered. Not unoften, when we pray for flowers, God sends us seeds. He gives us the gift of toil and labour, so that we may grow our own flowers.

There was a sister from Hong Kong, who came to see me in Pune. She was deeply disturbed by what she perceived as the deprivation, dirt, filth and chaos in India. "When I see this country with its poverty and the suffering of the people," she said to me, "my faith in God breaks down completely." True faith is unbreakable. It can never be broken. The problem with the lady was that she did not have faith.

Many of us have faith only in our ego self. When something happens which our ego self is not able to understand or grasp, we claim that our faith is broken – utterly and completely destroyed. Our prayers to God and the answers we receive from Him, often prove to be a test of our Faith.

To put it simply, there are four ways in which God answers our prayers. Many of us are apt to complain that our prayers have not been answered at all. This is not true. EVERY PRAYER IS ANSWERED. The trouble with us is, we fail to recognise the answer.

As I said, God answers our prayer in four ways:

> The first is "Yes." We ask for something; we pray to God, and He says, "Yes, my child. Here it is; I give you what you asked for."
> The second is "No." For a good reason, God tells us, "No, my child, I will not grant your prayer."
> The third is "Wait." It is as if God tells us that the time is not ripe for us to receive what we want. So He tells us, "Wait. The time is not yet."
> The fourth is, "Here is something better." We have asked for one thing, but He grants us something else and says, "Here is something different, something better that I want to give you."

When the answer is in the affirmative, when God says "Yes", we feel very happy. We praise God, we thank Him; we call Him a loving God, a wonderful God, and our faith in Him becomes stronger.

But the other three answers – "No", "Wait" and "Here is something better" – it is these three that test our faith.

When God says "No", the man of true faith believes that there is a meaning of mercy even in the negative answer. He says to himself, "If God does not want to give me this, it must be for my own good." It was Dean Inglow who said, "I have lived long enough to thank God for *not* having answered many of my prayers."

God loves us. He has a plan for each one of us; and His plans are perfect. If what we ask in prayer goes contrary to God's plan, that prayer is not granted – and of course, this is for our own good.

There was a woman who said, "I am grateful that God did not answer many of my prayers. When I was a college student, I fell in love with a man and fervently prayed that I might be married to him. Later, that man turned out to be drunkard, a gambler, a profligate. God said 'No' to my prayer, and I married a man who is a real gem of a human being."

Suppose a little child were to come up to its father and ask for a matchbox or for poison or a razor – will the father give any of these things to him? On the contrary, he would say, "No my child, I will not give it to you because it will harm you."

So too, there are certain things that God in His divine wisdom, denies to us. He never ever makes a mistake. He knows what is good for me, what is good for you, and He will grant us only that which is good for us, and nothing else. For each one of us, He has an individual plan, and it is a perfect plan. If what I ask for subscribes to that plan, He grants it to me, not otherwise.

> **On a long journey of human life, faith is the best of companions; it is the best refreshment on the journey; and it is the greatest property.**
> —*Gautama the Buddha*

Our wisdom is limited. We do not even know what will happen to us after five minutes. Yet we ask for things, which may actually cause us great harm in the future. God is all wisdom; God is all love. He is too loving to punish and too wise to make a mistake. Therefore, when He says "No", when He does not grant our prayer, we can be certain that it is for our highest good, our ultimate good.

In answer to some of our prayers, God says, "Wait." When God tells us to wait, there is great wisdom in it.

A boy of twelve asked his wealthy father for a Mercedes Benz. The father could very well afford such a car for his son; but for obvious reasons, he said to the son, "Wait, my child. I shall get the car for you when the right time comes."

In answer to some of our prayers, God says, "Here is something better!"

Columbus set out to find a shorter route to India. He prayed fervently for success in his venture. His prayers were answered with something better than finding a shorter route to India; Columbus became the world-famous discoverer of America.

Pasteur, the great French scientist, prayed that he might find a cure for a disease rampant among cattle. He discovered something far more valuable to human beings – a cure for rabies, the dreaded dog-madness disease.

Hindu philosophy, especially *Visishtadvaita*, emphasises the concept of *Sharanagati* – total surrender at the Lotus Feet of the Lord. Sri Krishna Himself tells us in the Gita:

> Renouncing all rites and writ duties, come to Me alone for single Refuge; do not fear, for I shall liberate thee from all bondage to sin and suffering. Of this have no doubt.

But this kind of surrender is not a matter of words uttered by the lips. It is an attitude of the heart. It requires total, absolute, unconditional faith. How many of us are capable of such faith?

Therefore, let me warn you, the way of faith is not a bed of roses; there are thorns too. Faith involves the spirit of acceptance; we must accept joys and sorrows, triumphs and failures, ups and downs; in the midst of these *dwandas* (binary opposites) we must still keep our faith intact! He who would walk the way of faith must be prepared to accept suffering and starvation, poverty and pain, and in the midst of it all, give gratitude to God.

> **The antidote to frustration is a calm faith, not in your own cleverness, or in hard toil, but in God's guidance.**
> *–Norman Vincent Peale*

The way of faith is not always easy. Life is a challenge, which must be met with the weapon of faith. Illness may come to you; death may stare you in the face; your dear ones may let you down when you need their support desperately. You may have to face storms of misunderstanding. Disappointments may crowd around you. Your friends may scoff at you, laugh behind your back and call you a fool. Occasionally, they may even taunt you, "Where is your God?" And, in the day of your anguish and misery, you yourself may say, in the heart within, "I can bear it no longer! I am broken in body, mind and spirit! In this big, wide world, there is none whom I can call my own. I feel forsaken as a beaten, battered boat on a stormy sea! Not this path for me!"

If you survive this period of despair and frustration — and believe me, you can do so through constant prayer and repetition of the Name of God — you arrive at a stage of blessedness. Your struggles will be over. With you it will no longer be a matter of hope or faith or trust — it will be a matter of knowledge. You begin to *know* that you are in God's hands and that He will provide for you at the right place, at the right time!

Swami Vivekananda was traveling aboard a steamer that was taking him to America to attend the World Congress of Religions. Although a kind benefactor had purchased the ticket for his voyage, no arrangements had been made for his stay in the United States. There would be no one to receive him on his arrival in that strange, new land. He did not know where he would go when he disembarked, nor where he would stay. However, he *did* know one thing for certain: that the Great Providence, who had always taken care of him, would not let him down in that distant land to which he was now being sent.

As the Swami stood on the deck communing with the Lord of love in the heart within, a fellow passenger came to greet him. The Swami's radiant face and piercing eyes had fascinated the American, who was eager to get to know him.

"What takes you to America?" he asked Swamiji, when they had shaken hands and introduced themselves to each other.

"I go to attend the World Congress of Religions which is to be held in Chicago," the Swami replied.

"I am from Chicago," the man said. "May I know where you will stay when you are in Chicago?"

This was more than Swami Vivekanada knew. "I do not know," he said, adding, with his dazzling smile, "may be, I shall stay at your place?"

The words were uttered in such childlike simplicity that they went right to the heart of this wealthy man from Chicago. Without a moment's hesitation, he said, "It will be a joy and privilege to have someone like you staying in my house. I shall endeavour to keep you as comfortable as I can!"

Many of us are willing and eager to lay our trust in God — but only up to a point. Our trust is partial because our experience keeps us tied down to men and material possessions. The body needs food day after day and so we must always have a stock of food in the house. Prices go up and scarcity may arise, so we hoard things which may not be easily available. We need so many other things which can be bought only with money — and so we must have savings in the bank. The banks may crash — so we buy stocks and shares and gold.

Alas, we forget that all these are unreliable — but there is One who abideth forever. He was, He is, and He always will be for ever and ever more. He is the Giver of all that is. He is the Sustainer of all life. Out of Him is all that we see and all that we hold. And it is His Will that works in all the world and the galaxies of planets and stars.

This kind of faith – the state of utter self surrender in which a man possesses nothing, and himself is God-possessed, is not possible for the majority of mankind. It is too far advanced a stage and is arrived at only after a person has passed through many a trial of faith. The majority of men will tell me: "I have a family to look after; I have to earn my livelihood. I have to provide for the education of my children, I have to pay the doctor's bills, house-rent and taxes. What can I do? What must I do?

Is it not true that we often imagine God being deaf, dumb and blind to our miserable cries for help? "Comforter, where is thy comfort?" we call, in the words of the poet. Little do we realise that He is there *with* us, working *through* us, to perform His miracles. We may not see how He works, but He is sure to help us out of our suffering. It is this profound truth that is expressed in the words of the Lord in the Gita: *Know this for certainty, Arjuna: My devotee is never lost.* All we have to do is cling to Him in faith and hope: He will not, indeed He *cannot* let us down!

There are terrible problems confronting the world today – starvation, poverty, war, violence, religious fanaticism, environmental degradation and more! It is enough to depress the most optimistic among us. And so, even good people exclaim in despair – "What can we do? How much can we do? Whatever we do, it's not going to be enough!"

> **Faith isn't the ability to believe long and far into the misty future.**
> **It's simply taking God at His Word and taking the next step.**
> *–Joni Erickson Tada*

True – it may not be enough. But that should be no reason for us to desist from all action. Rather, we must do what we can, in the firm faith and belief, "I *can* make a difference! I *will* make a difference."

Charles Andrews was a young man who had dedicated his life to God very early in life. He decided to go among the people of a notorious locality in London – for he wished to serve them in all sincerity and devotion.

Criminals, cheats, rogues and drunkards thronged the locality day and night. Charles Andrews saw a man staggering out of a tavern, dead drunk.

"Look here, friend. You must stop drinking," Andrews said to him, as he helped him get on to the pavement. The drunkard pushed Charles away, and hurled the most vile abuses against him.

"Oh Lord Christ, forgive this man and bless him," prayed Andrews.

This became a daily occurrence. One day, the drunkard said to Andrews, "You are an absolute fool if you think God will ever forgive me!" He added morosely, "And besides, I have no trust in Him."

"My friend, my brother!" said Andrews with infinite compassion. "Whether you have faith in the Lord or not, He has full faith in you! A day will come when you will surely give up drinking!"

"You think so?" asked the drunkard. "Are you sure God has faith in me?"

"I assure you He does!" Andrews told him.

The man turned over a new leaf. He left drinking from that day.

Charles Andrews, when he came to India later, became known as *Dinabandhu* – for he served poor people as if he were their own brother.

Believe that with God, all things are possible! Many doctors have assured us that they have seen men, after all therapy had failed, lifted out of affliction and disease by the serene effect of faith. Faith, indeed, seems to overcome even the so-called 'laws of nature'. And the occasions on which prayer has dramatically done this have been termed 'miracles'.

Trust in the Lord! In faith, you achieve harmony of body, mind and spirit which gives unshakeable strength to your weakest efforts. Did not Jesus say, "Ask and it shall be given to you?" True, faith cannot bring the dead back to life, or wipe away pain and suffering. But faith, like radium, is a source of luminous energy that can light up our lives.

> **God is even kinder than you think.**
> *–St Theresa*

As human beings, we seek to augment our finite energy by linking ourselves to God, who is the Source of infinite energy. His power is inexhaustible, and He is ready to give it to us. Just by asking for His help, our deficiencies are set right and we are restored, rejuvenated and strengthened. With Him, all things are possible!

By myself, I can do nothing: that is the very first principle of spiritual life. The second principle is – He that is within you is greater than he that is outside. To us, external forces appear to be strong and powerful. But they are nothing compared to that which is within you – the Lord, who is seated in the throne of your heart, for whom everything is possible.

Significant are the words of the great German mystic, Meister Eckhart: "Where creature stops, there God begins. All God wants of thee is to go out of thyself in respect of thy creatureliness and let God be the God-in-thee."

Let God take over our lives, for He makes the impossible possible!

> **No matter how steep the mountain - the Lord is going to climb it with you.**
> *—Helen Steiner Rice*

Of course there are bound to be several people who would argue, "How is it possible to hand things over to God and just sit back? Just look at the world we live in! It's a terrible place. Consider the times we live in – these are troubled and disturbing times. And we are confronted by problems wherever we turn!"

My answer to them is this: God has faith in us, and He knows that troubles can make us better, stronger human beings. When we hand our troubles and cares over to Him in a spirit of surrender, He will bring about the change that we need most.

The great statistician, Babson, once said "The greatest undeveloped resource of the world, is faith. And the greatest unused power is prayer." True it is that faith is a tremendous resource – but, alas, it is an unused treasure. And, the question is, why don't we pray? Why don't we put to good use our greatest resource?

What we need, above all else today is the rediscovery of the great truth that God *is* - that He is real; that we need to renew our faith in Him.

Epictetus once said, "There is only one way to happiness and that is to cease worrying about things which are beyond the power of our will."

I can hear many of you murmuring, "Cease worrying! Easier said than done!"

It is in the nature of the mind to worry. I doubt whether any of us ever go to bed without having worried about something or the other during the day. But many of us worry about imaginary problems. I feel the mind has two enemies which can undermine our functioning: one is worry and the other is fear. The two together, I think, can actually destroy a human being. As Samuel Ullman says, "Years may wrinkle the skin, but to give up enthusiasm wrinkles the soul. Worry, fear, self-distrust bows the heart and turns the spirit back to dust."

A woman came to me sometime ago. She had a problem. She was blessed with everything an ordinary human being could possibly desire: but she simply could not bring herself to sit in silence and meditate. She had a good home and a family, a loving and caring husband, and obedient children who respected her every wish. How many women are so fortunate? Yet, her main problem was worry. Whenever she found time, (which was quite often), she would sit down to meditate. But the moment she sat down, all kinds of worries would begin to gnaw at her mind. She said to me, "I try to use my reason and comfort myself. Yet, my mind does not stop worrying. What should I do?"

I said to her, "The best antidote to worry is faith. To dispel your worry, all you need to do is chant the Name Divine. Just sing, *Re Maan Tu Kyun Chinta Kare? Dhyan Hari Ka Kyun Na Dhare* – O mind, why do you keep worrying? Why don't you stay and meditate on God?"

O mind, why do you worry? Easy to ask that question, but difficult to find the answer! But, left to itself, untrained, undisciplined and uncontrolled, it is the nature of the mind to churn out worries and brew fear. Worry is the malignancy which eats away the insides of a man. What is the cure for worrying? The cure for worrying is faith. Where there is faith, there can no worry, because faith is an illumination, faith is light. Worry, on the other hand, is darkness. Where there is light there cannot be darkness. Therefore we must learn to dispel all worries with the light of faith.

A famous man once observed, "I believe God is managing our affairs and that He doesn't need any advice from me. With God in charge, I believe everything will work out for the best in the end. So what is there to worry about?" Can you guess who it was? It was not a priest, not a renunciate, but a hard headed industrialist, and one of the outstanding entrepreneurs of his time, Henry Ford, who made this statement.

There was a sister who was under tremendous pressure both at work and on the home front. The company she worked for was passing through a financial crisis, and was severely short-staffed, with each employee doing the work of two or three people. There was no question of complaining, because she knew she was lucky to have a job, while a dozen others like her had lost theirs. At home, she had an old mother to care for and a younger brother and sister to support. Sometimes, she said, she was overwhelmed by the thought of what lay ahead for her when she awoke in the morning.

I taught her a simple prayer. Every morning, as she awoke, I told her to hand her day over to the Lord and tell Him, "Lord, this day is Thine, and all the work I do, I offer to you. I know I cannot carry the load myself. I hand my life over to you. I beg you to get everything done for me."

She found a miraculous change in her life. Everything seemed to fall into place; her burdens seemed to lift of their own accord. Everything seemed – just more manageable!

The secret of true faith is in three words: "Let it go!" Let it go! Let God! Let go of your fears, your guilt, your problems and your frustrations. Let go in God's name! For He is the Support and Sustenance of your life. There are no obstacles on your path that He cannot clear; no problems that He, in His mercy and Wisdom cannot solve!

How can we cultivate such faith? So let me pass on to you a few practical suggestions:

1. The first essential thing is a change of outlook. As it is, we depend too much on ourselves, our efforts and endeavours. We keep God out of the picture. True, human effort has its place in life. But we need to understand that above all efforts is His Will. And He is the Giver of all that is! So let not our work be egotistic— but dedicated. Let us learn to work as His agents, the instruments of His Will. Our children are His children. We are here to serve them to the best of our ability and capacity. It is His responsibility to provide for them— may be through us, or others. And His coffers are ever full!

2. The second essential thing is to share what we have with others. Therefore let us set apart a portion—say one-tenth of our earnings to be utilized in the service of God and His suffering creation.

To those who are unable to live on their income, this may appear a difficult thing to do. But even they will find that in the measure in which they share what little they have with others, they will be richly blessed. Out of the little that remains to them, they will get more, much more than they expected. This is what we, in the Sindhi language, call *barkat*.

I know a lady in Australia who sets apart a tenth of her earnings for just such a purpose – and she has not been the poorer for it. Once, when she sent a certain amount to be spent on the service activities of our Sadhu Vaswani Mission, she wrote to me, "It is with gratitude that I pass on to you this amount from my 'Lord's Tenth' fund. This money has nothing to do with me, except that I send it to wherever the Lord directs. So this gift is from Him and the recognition and thanks are due to Him….

This is one of the laws of life – the more we give, the more we get out of the little that remains.

3. Do not be scared of anything. Trust in the Lord and face the battle of life. There is no power on earth that can lay you low.

4. Trust in Him. Turn to Him for everything you need. Make Him your Senior Partner – and success will flow into your life as rivers flow into the sea!

5. We must contact God again and again. It is necessary for us to repeat His name again and again to pray without ceasing. A prayer which may prove helpful is, "Lord! Make me a channel of Thy mercy!"

6. To become a channel of His mercy, we must surrender all we are and all we have, at His Lotus-feet. So may we become His instruments of help and healing in this world of suffering and pain.

He who hath surrendered himself hath found the greatest security of life. And we need wander no more. All his cares and burdens are borne by the Lord Himself. How beautiful are the words of the Gita:

> They who worship Me
> Depending on Me alone,
> Thinking of no other—
> They are My sole responsibility!
> Their burdens are My burdens!
> To them I bring full security!

The more we meditate on the Lord's words, the more we shall grow in that true life which is a life of self-surrender. The life of faith is a blessed, carefree life. It is a life free from the shackles of earthly "experience". To be truly free is to be born anew, to become a pure child of God. Such a one lives with God and walks with God and speaks to Him and hears Him speak.

• • • • • • •

If a man has not learnt to be patient,
he has learnt very little.

J. P. Vaswani

• • • • • • •

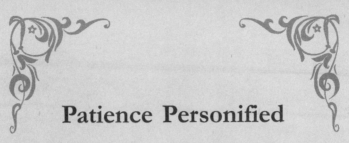

Patience Personified

Sant Eknath was a picture of patience. He was always unruffled and serene — a saint who never lost his temper. There were some men in the town who were jealous of his reputation and were eager to prove to the people that Sant Eknath, too, had feet of clay. They hired a man and promised to reward him richly, if only he could make the saint lose his temper.

Early every morning, Eknath would go to the river for a dip in the waters before spending some time in worship. One day, as he returned to his cottage, after taking a bath in the sacred waters, on the way, the hired man spat on him.

Quietly, the saint went back to the river and took a dip for the second time.

Once again, as he was on his way home, the man spat on him. The same thing happened again and again. The thought of the rich reward lured the man and he kept spitting on the saint every time that he passed by him. As for the saint, his patience and composure did not waver in the least.

Believe it or not, this went on for as many as 107 times! After taking the 108th dip, as the saint wended his way home, the man's heart melted. Falling at the feet of the saint, he sobbed, " For the sake of God, do forgive me! I have sinned greatly. I was told by some of the wealthy men of the town that if I could only make you lose your patience and force you to give way to bad temper, they would reward me handsomely. The temptation of a rich reward made me stoop this low! Pray forgive me!"

Lifting him up, the saint smiled and said, "Forgive you, for what? Today is a unique day in my life, when I have had 108 dips in the sacred river! Had you only told me of the rich reward promised to you, I would have gladly feigned impatience and anger for your benefit!"

6

THE FIFTH GATEWAY TO HEAVEN: PATIENCE

There are many virtues which can be cultivated by means of other virtues: thus, love leads you on to compassion; compassion leads you on to selflessness and service of the suffering ones; faith gives you hope; truth gives you honesty and integrity. But you need a lot of patience to learn the wonderful virtue of patience!

Let us begin our approach to this – the fifth gateway to heaven – by understanding the root meaning of the word patience. The Dictionary defines it as: the quality of being patient, as in the bearing of provocation, annoyance, misfortune, or pain, *without complaint, loss of temper, irritation, or the like.*

Patience in daily life is an ability or willingness to suppress restlessness or annoyance when confronted with delay: such as a good teacher who has patience with a slow learner.

'Patience' is also used to refer to quiet, steady perseverance; even-tempered care; and also diligence: we praise people who work with patience.

May I say the synonyms for the word 'patience' in the English language are even more revealing: composure, stability, self-possession; submissiveness, sufferance, endurance, fortitude, stoicism, all of which imply qualities of calmness, stability, and persistent courage in trying circumstances. Patience also denotes calm, self-possessed, and uncomplaining bearing of pain, misfortune, annoyance, or delay. And finally, 'patience' also refers to indefatigability, persistence, assiduity.

As we may see, Patience is not just *a* virtue, it is a compendium of several good qualities.

Have you heard of the beautiful prayer, "God, give me the power to change the things I can, accept the things that I cannot change, and the wisdom to know the difference?"

> **Where there is charity and wisdom, there is neither fear nor ignorance. Where there is patience and humility, there is neither anger nor vexation. Where there is poverty and joy, there is neither greed nor avarice. Where there is peace and meditation, there is neither anxiety nor doubt.**
> *–St. Francis*

Alas, we spend much of our time and energy trying to control things which we cannot control. The futile effort leaves us frustrated, impatient and embittered. We need to develop the virtues of patience and acceptance – not as passive, helpless victims, but as wise and understanding human beings.

Tolerance, understanding, acceptance: the world has great need of these today. Above all, we need to be patient with ourselves!

Patience is essential for every aspirant who wishes to make progress on the spiritual path. In this, as in so many other things, Nature is our best teacher. If only we observe Mother Nature, if only we would appreciate her splendid panorama in all its wondrous magic, we would perceive that nature does not hurry, it is never in haste, and everything happens in its due course. Look at the sun, it religiously rises in the morning and sets in the evening. This has gone on for centuries, and it will continue to do so for centuries to come. The sun keeps shining, giving its light to the earth and sustaining all the creatures on it. The sun never changes its course; it never fails in its task of affording light and warmth to us.

> **Both in this work-a-day world as well as in the spiritual sphere, patience is the crown of life.**
> *—Anandamayi Ma*

Likewise, the trees stand firm in sunshine and rain. The trees do not complain, in fact they bless us by providing us with shade, fuel, wood and fruit. A tree is invaluable to man. And yet we pay no attention to its presence or indeed acknowledge the many benefits we receive from it.

When we read the life of Sri Dattatreya, we learn that the Earth taught him the qualities of patience, forbearance and doing good to others.

From the moment we get up from sleep, we stand upon the earth, we stamp upon it, we tread upon it, we jump and walk upon it. The earth puts up with it all – it puts up with billions upon billions of people like us and continues to support us. The trees that grow upon the earth share this quality with their earth mother. They provide shelter and fruits to everyone – even to those who throw stones at them.

The true seeker learns to cultivate endurance, compassion and selflessness from the earth.

Very often I have heard people complain that they work very hard, but do not receive adequate reward or recognition for their efforts. Once I met a man who was perhaps going through the same experience. He said that whenever he felt his efforts were unappreciated, he would go to an area where men were laying new roads. Here, he would watch the labourers breaking stones, tirelessly. These men keep hammering the stones in order to break them into rubble. The labourers keep on at this back-breaking work ceaselessly. They continued with the drudgery of breaking stones day in and day out for a pittance, which is often barely enough to feed their large families. Their patience and untiring, uncomplaining effort, is something that spiritual seekers would do well to emulate.

Let me add, patience is a great virtue; it helps us to grow on the spiritual path; but this path, as we all know, is difficult. It has many obstacles. Without patience we would never be able to tread this path. Even for those of us who do not aspire to spiritual progress, patience is vital in our daily dealings. With patience one can solve one's own problems and help others as well. Patience brings rhythm and harmony into our chaotic lives. And as we saw, Mother Nature too follows the law of patience in her ceaseless cycles and steady rhythm.

In this world of haste and waste, stress and tension, trials and tribulations, patience assumes a great worth. Patience is necessary to avoid dissipating our energies. Patience makes life smooth and stress-free.

Gautama the Buddha had a worthy disciple. This disciple decided to leave the *ashram* one day, in order to seek self-realisation. He resolved that unless and until he achieved this goal, he would not return to the *ashram*. He felt it was essential to be on his own, so that he could meditate on his inner self and perhaps, reach the goal. Living with other disciples in the *ashram* appeared to him as an obstacle on the spiritual path. Hence, he sought solitude in order to work his way to *nirvana*.

Being alone, without the company of those on the spiritual path, can sometimes have a negative effect. The intense loneliness of the mind can give vent to suppressed desires. This is exactly what happened to this *bikshu*. All kinds of evil thoughts troubled his mind. He lost his sanguine and pious nature. After years of fruitless effort, he returned to the *ashram* without accomplishing his task.

The inmates of the *ashram* asked him, "Have you found the truth?" The *bikshu* replied cynically, "There is no truth. I wish to give up this pursuit of knowledge and go and live in the world as an ordinary person." The others tried to convince him that he should not leave the path midway, but pursue his spiritual journey with renewed devotion and patience. They further impressed upon him the need to meet the Master. They took him to Gautama the Buddha.

Mahatma Buddha said, "O son, why do you want to give up so easily? Why have you lost your patience?" The *bikshu* was unable to answer. Mahatma Buddha held him in his powerful gaze of illumination, for a minute. Then he said to him, "O dear one, do not lose patience so easily. There was a time when you saved five hundred lives. Why do you despair now?"

> **If I have ever made any valuable discoveries, it has been owing more to patient attention, than to any other talent.**
> —*Isaac Newton*

Hearing this, the *bikshu* weeps. He repents his decision to leave the *ashram*. The words of Gautama the Buddha restore his faith in life. The *bikshus* of the *ashram* are surprised. They humbly ask the Master, "How did he save five hundred lives?"

Mahatma Buddha smiles and says to them, "He is known to you only for a few years. But I have known him from many lives. In one of his previous births he was the servant of a well-to-do merchant. Once, the merchant loaded his caravan and went to trade in a neighbouring country. The merchant's caravan had five hundred people and nearly as many camels. The caravan had to cross a desert. The journey through the desert was to take 28 days. The caravan had a guide who showed the way through the desert. As the desert was very hot and inhospitable the caravan moved during the night and rested during the day, pitching their tents to shield themselves from the blistering desert sun. The caravan had carried food and water only for 28 days. On the 27th day the ration of the food and water was over, but the merchant thought to himself that they would surely reach their destination within 24 hours.

As fate or fortune would have it, it so happened that on the night of the 28th day, the guide was sleepy and tired. He misguided the caravan so that it travelled in the wrong direction. Next morning, when the sun rose the merchant realised that they had reached the same place where they had pitched their tents the previous day. Exhausted and thirsty, the merchant was at a loss, as to how he would provide food and water to his people, who were under his care, and his moral responsibility. However, he had great faith in God. He prayed to God fervently, and sought his help. Suddenly he noticed at a distance, a spot of green, underneath a giant stone. "There should be some water over there", he mused. The merchant's men started digging around the stone but could not find water. The merchant pressed his ear to the stone and he could hear the rustle of running water. He called his servant and asked him to break the stone. As the servant broke the stone, water trickled out from the seams. The merchant's men were happy. The sight of water infused a new life in them. They quenched their thirst with the cool waters of the stone and also used it for bathing.

Mahatma Buddha said, "In that life, I was that merchant and this *bikshu* was my servant, who broke the stone and saved the lives of five hundred men."

Let us not give up our effort on the spiritual path. Let us not lose courage, but cultivate the virtue of patience, and face the challenges of life with equanimity and fortitude. Let us continue with our *sadhana* and with our prayers.

> **There art two cardinal sins from which all others spring: Impatience and Laziness.**
> —*Franz Kafka*

I am sure you have heard of St. Augustine. He was born of a noble family. Unfortunately, he got into bad company and began to live a sinful life. He actually began to live with a concubine. His parents lived in a different city. When they come to know of his sinful ways, they felt miserable. His mother, a pious and devoted Christian, wept and prayed to the Lord to save her son and redeem him from his sinful ways. "O Lord, grant him a new life", she kept praying – not for a day, a week or a month but for years together. Her son showed no signs of remorse or repentance; but she was patient and persistent in her prayers; she was a woman of faith and believed that her prayers would be answered. After very, many years there was a remarkable transformation in Augustine's life and he became a saint of God.

So let me urge you, do not lose patience easily, be strong willed. Cultivate the strength within. Do not be irritated by minor irrelevant incidents, do not waste your energies on futile discussions and debates. Let there be no war of words that drain you of all energy. Keep your mind under control and focus your thoughts on things that ought to be.

Patience is not a passive virtue, as some people think. Patience, as experts are now beginning to understand, is a 'proactive choice' and a vital way of perseverance that keeps you moving towards your goal. The lives of the great ones bear ample testimony to this.

Let me tell you about the first Revelation that was given to Lord Zarathustra. In this vision, he perceived Ahura Mazda as the Wise Lord of Creation, and the six emanations of Ahura Mazda, the *Amesha Spentas*, as the guardians and artisans of this physical world. He perceived the laws upon which the universe operated, and understood the inter-relationship between Ahura Mazda, the *Amesha Spentas*, and the Creation.

> **Have patience with all things, but chiefly have patience with yourself. Do not lose courage in considering your own imperfections but instantly set about remedying them – every day begin the task anew.**
> *–Saint Francis de Sales*

For the next ten years, he moved through the towns and the villages of his native land, proclaiming the Truth that had been revealed to him. Not once did he get an eager, receptive audience, willing to listen to him. The people were just not ready to receive from the Prophet the revelation meant for them and the rest of mankind. He was greeted with jeers and howls wherever he went; they even pelted stones at him, inflicting wounds on his pure, sacred body. He bore in gentle and loving patience the pain and the scorn heaped upon him. On his lips was the smile of mercy and in his heart was the prayer: "O Ahura Mazda! Have mercy on them and lead them out of the darkness of the Evil One, into the Light of Thy Truth!"

As we know, the scoffers and disbelievers could not stop Zoroaster from his ordained path: his followers grew in number, and they gave the Master their undying loyalty and commitment. To this day, the Parsis in India retain his qualities of patience and gentleness!

Patience is the alchemist who turns every blow into a blessing, every burden into a benediction. As the pilgrim moves on the Path, he is tried and tested, as gold is tested by being thrown into the crucible. Significant are the words of Hudayafa al-Yaman, "When God loves a servant, He proves him by suffering." If he is patient, he will not avoid suffering, but will greet it with a smile, knowing that all that comes from God is good.

The man of patience thrives on suffering: the more he suffers, the more his soul shines. The great Sufi teacher and mystic, Jalal ud-Din Rumi, unfolds a very beautiful picture in his *Masnavi*. He writes, "There is an animal called the porcupine. It is made stout and big by blows of the stick. The more you cudgel it, the more it thrives. The soul of a true believer is, verily, a porcupine. The more it is chastised, the more it thrives. So it is that God's chosen ones have to bear a greater share of suffering than other worldly men. Suffering gives strength to their souls."

And if you have had to pass through a period of pain and suffering, I assure you, God will not let you suffer in vain: you must remember, God always acts at the right time and if He does not act, it only means that the right time is not yet come.

There are situations in everyday life that tax our patience; waiting in the immigration/customs queue to obtain your entry permit; trying to acquire a license or special permission from a government department; being stuck in a traffic jam; even standing in line to obtain an application form for your child's nursery admission – life seems excessively stressful!

> # A handful of patience is worth more than a bushel of brains.
> *—Dutch Proverb*

Let me tell you the story of a patient, kind and courteous man, who lived in those days when telephones were uncommon and each call you made had to be connected through the telephone exchange. You could not dial any number directly in those days. The telephone operator at the 'exchange' would ask for the number and then key it into her 'board' and make the connection for the call. Once, a man asked the telephone operator to give him a particular number. By mistake, the telephone operator connected him to a wrong number. The man very gently told the telephone operator that she had given him the wrong connection. At this, the telephone operator apologised to him and said she would dial the right number for him. As luck would have it, she connected him to the wrong number the second time. The third time, this man cautioned the telephone operator and requested her to be more attentive while dialing the number. He explained that his call was urgent. But for the third time also, she gave him a wrong connection!

This happened seven times. When the caller made the request for the eighth time, the telephone operator was surprised and touched. Actually, she had been told that her father had had a sudden heart attack and was shifted to the ICCU of a Heart Institute. She was therefore unable to concentrate on her work; in her stress and anxiety, every time she dialed the number it went to the wrong party.

The telephone operator said to the gentleman, "Sir, you have great patience. You talk so courteously and gently, even after I have given you the wrong number seven times. How is it that you are so kind?"

The gentleman replied, 'I have received this gift of patience from my Guru.'

'Who is your Guru?'

'Would you like to attend his *satsang* and listen to his discourses?' he asked her.

'Certainly,' she replied, 'I would love to hear the sacred words of a Guru, whose disciple is so gentle, that he forgave my mistakes seven times and retained his patience as well as his soft and sweet voice for the eighth time! If the disciple is so sweet and gentle, his Guru must be truly great.'

Communication experts tell us that among the younger generation, listening is perhaps the most neglected of skills. Evidence shows that many people have problems with listening. This is not because they are deaf or hard of hearing; it is just that they are rather inefficient as listeners. We miss much of what is said and forget much of what we hear. Experts say we retain only 25% of what we hear after 2 days! Here are some of their other findings:

- Listening is the weakest link in oral communication.

- In most organisations, about 50% of the time is spent in listening. Managers are thought to spend 9% of their time writing, 16% of their time reading, 30% of their time speaking, and 45% of their time just listening to others. And yet, most people feel that not enough attention is paid to their needs, their problems and grievances!

- Most of us do not have any fundamental hearing deficiency– still we do not listen very well.

Experts also point out that impatience is one of the worst barriers to listening. People have no patience to let the other person finish what he has to say. They want to interrupt, add their own comments or narrate their own experiences.

Such competitive barrier indicates a lack of maturity. We must cultivate patience and courtesy, at least to the extent of allowing the speaker to finish whatever he has to say.

"Patience is bitter, but its fruit is sweet," said Rousseau. Anger is the killer of patience – it can destroy, demolish patience utterly.

The story is told us of the weaver saint Thiruvalluvar of South India, that a cheeky young man once came to buy a *saree* from him. In truth, he had come to provoke the saint beyond the point of endurance – to prove that the saint was only human!

"How much does this *saree* cost?" he asked, picking up a valuable *saree*.

The saint named the price.

"And this?" said the young man, tearing the *saree* in two.

The saint halved his price.

"And now?" the youth continued, tearing up the half-*saree* into two.

Thus it went on, the youth tearing the *saree* into pieces until it was reduced to the width of a small rag – and the saint remaining calm and quiet in the face of such deliberate provocation.

The young man was overcome with repentance as he saw the beautiful *saree* reduced to useless bits. "I beg your pardon sir," he said to the saint, "Let me pay you the price of the whole *saree*."

"No, you need not," said the saint. "The pieces are useless to you. In any case the hard work and effort that went to make that *saree* are invaluable. You cannot pay for *that*!"

"But it was my arrogance and stupidity which destroyed the *saree*," pleaded the young man.

"I can weave another *saree* like that easily" said the saint. "But if your life is torn apart by such actions, it cannot be mended!"

The saint did not mind his personal loss and the insults he had to bear. His concern was for the young man's spiritual welfare. Sure enough, his blessings transformed the life of the young man.

The weaver-saint was not merely doing his duty as a honest weaver – refusing to accept money for a torn sari, which would be of no use to anyone. He also went one step further—for he was able to see into the mind of the rude young man, and realized that he needed motivation to change. The saint did not mind the loss he had incurred, or the insult meted out to him. With his tremendous patience and tact, he had dealt with a recalcitrant youth so effectively as to cure him of his negative traits.

Many people today, lose patience with their employers and quit their jobs – only to regret the rash decision later, when they find it difficult to obtain a new position. A little patience and tolerance could have saved them from the insecurity of unemployment. I always tell my friends, that they must abide in patience, until the way before them is clear.

Are you one of those people who is dissatisfied with your environment?

Remember, you are the right person in the right place, learning the right lesson at the right time.

When you have learnt it, out of the very depths of life will sound the words: "Move on!"

And the conditions around you will change, and you will find yourself in a new environment!

All it takes is patience.

Once, Mahatma Gandhi was travelling by train from Champaran to Bekhiyanagar. There were many people travelling with him. They all occupied the seats in the compartment but left a whole berth for Mahatma Gandhi. Mahatma Gandhi had been on his walking trail since morning, and he was very tired. His followers requested him to lie down on the empty berth. Mahatma Gandhi agreed to occupy the berth and soon he fell asleep. After a few hours, a rustic farmer entered the compartment at a wayside station. Seeing a man sleeping on the berth he lost his patience. He rudely shook up Mahatma Gandhi, quarrelling with him and telling him harshly, that he had no business to occupy the full berth for himself, in a compartment that was so overcrowded. Mahatma Gandhi immediately sat up and gave place to the farmer. As the train moved, the man started singing the patriotic songs made popular all over the country by Gandhiji's followers. He also started shouting slogans in favour of Mahatma Gandhi. Mahatma Gandhi watched all this in silence and smiled.

The rustic farmer was actually going to Bekhiyanagar to have a *darshan* of Mahatma Gandhi and so he was singing heroic songs and shouting slogans, praising Mahatma Gandhi. In the morning, when the train reached Bekhiyanagar, loud cheering could be heard, "*Mahatma Gandhi ki jai*!" The station platform was crowded. People from all walks of life had gathered there to welcome Mahatma Gandhi. It was then that the farmer realised that the man he had abused and been rough with was none other than Mahatma Gandhi himself. The poor man began to cry and fell at Gandhiji's feet. Gandhiji immediately lifted him up and embraced him. The Mahatma had shown what it was to be patient, understanding and egoless. Although he was insulted and abused by the rustic farmer, he had maintained silence and remained calm and peaceful.

I often tell my friends that the greatest famine in the world today is the famine of understanding; no two people seem to be able to understand each other. You will agree with me when I say that it is only the spirit of understanding that can foster good human relationships: and without patience and tolerance, how can we cultivate the spirit of understanding?

It was Zoroaster who said: "Know ye well, that a hundred temples of wood and stone have not the value of one single understanding heart!"

The word 'understanding' requires us to 'stand under' others. Alas, no one is prepared today to stand under anyone. Everybody wants to stay over everybody else. People have no patience with others. This is the main cause of misunderstandings.

A man was seen in the supermarket pushing a pram with a baby in it.

"Be patient, George," said the man looking at the pram.

"Be quiet, George," continued the man.

A nearby shopper came up to the man to tell him how much he admired the man's patience; after all it is not very easy to go shopping with a child in a pram. To this the man replied, very sheepishly, "I'm telling myself these things, not the baby in the pram. Actually, I'm George, nice meeting you."

My friends say to me that this is the age of instant solutions, instant foods and instant cash: no one has the patience to wait, leave alone cultivate the virtue of patience!

But I must point out to them, that the best things in life are achieved only after you have put in hard work and waited patiently for your efforts to bear fruit!

Patience can and must be cultivated by all of us, and I would like to offer you some practical suggestions for the same.

1. Avoid doing things in haste. "Multi-tasking" is a much valued attribute today; but in earlier, more relaxed times, we believed in the saying: "One thing at a time, and that done well…". Make a list of tasks to be completed, and go about each one systematically, taking the help of others if it is available.

2. Change your attitude to life and people, so that you may overcome stress and irritation. When your attitude is constructive and helpful, you automatically become more patient and understanding with people around you.

3. In this as in other things, acceptance is crucial to peace and harmony. Realise that there are some things in your life which are not under your control, and that you cannot change everything and everyone around you to suit your way of functioning.

4. Learn to relax consciously in stressful situations. Deep breathing is an instant de-stressor. In the long run, meditation also helps you to become stable, calm and patient.

5. When a situation becomes impossible for you to handle, learn to let go. Let go, let go, let God.

6. Remember, good things may not always come to people who wait, but very few good things in life come straightaway to any one!

7. Learn to take a break. Discover at least twice a week the joy of doing nothing – absolutely NO thing!

8. Get your priorities right. Ultimately, peace and good will are far more important than instant gratification of your desires. Take time to live! Take time to offer kindness and understanding to people around you, and create peace in your environment by being kind, tolerant, patient and understanding.

· · · · · · · · · ·

One way to keep away from the allurements
of the world is to attend *satsang* regularly.
Satsang is a place of hope and serenity; it is a
place of positive vibrations, which protects us
from the negativity of the world. The
temptations of the world are many and the
allurement of the world is powerful.
Anytime it can drag us into the whirlwind
of pleasure, pelf, worry.

J. P. Vaswani

· · · · · · · · · ·

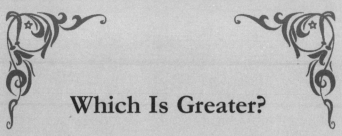

Which Is Greater?

Once, a debate took place between the two great sages Vashishta and Vishwamitra on the subject of, 'The Path to Spirituality'. *Rishi* Vishwamitra was of the view that *tapsaya* was the true path to spirituality. He said, "*Tapsaya* is *the* path. It is the true strength." However, *Rishi* Vashishta disagreed and said, "*Satsang* is the right path to self realisation. It is the best because it is easy." The debate went on and on. They simply could not come to an agreement. Hence, both of them decided to approach Mother Earth to give Her decision.

According to our ancient scriptures, the earth stands on the horns of a bull. This bull is the incarnation of compassion. The two *rishis* went to the bull and asked him, "Which is greater – *satsang* or *tapsaya*?" The bull replied that he would be able to give his decision, only if one of them would take over the burden of the earth from his horns. *Rishi* Vishwamitra was quick to answer, "Let me take the burden of this earth, while you take time off to make your decision." *Rishi* Vishwamitra tried to lift the earth. He said, "Whatever *tapsaya* I have done, I surrender here and now, so that I get enough strength to carry the earth on my shoulders." But, he could not do it. He cried out, "Ah...! All my strength is gone. I'm collapsing. I cannot take the burden of this Earth."

Now it was the turn of *Rishi* Vashishta to take on the burden of the Earth. *He* said, "Of all the time I have spent in *satsang*, in gathering spiritual strength, I surrender just a part of it here to be able to bear the burden of Mother Earth." So saying, he lifted the earth effortlessly and carried it, waiting for the answer.

The bull said to them, "You have the answer already. Look at Sage Vashishta, he has surrendered only a fraction of the *shakti* that he has gathered in the *satsang* and yet he is carrying the burden of Mother Earth. He has unlimited *shakti*."

Satsang generates tremendous *shakti*.

THE SIXTH GATEWAY TO HEAVEN: SATSANG

Have you ever wondered what is the noblest thing on the earth? Let me answer, in the words of my Gurudev, "The noblest work is to cultivate the soul." To cultivate the soul we should sow the seeds of love, selfless service and devotion. We should chant the Name Divine, set apart time for silent communion with God, and offer the service of love to those who are less fortunate than we are. We will then experience divinity in our everyday life.

I can hear some of my friends exclaim: "Chant the name divine? Set apart time for silent communion? Dada, we are not renunciates and ascetics! We are men of the world, and we have businesses, careers and families to worry about. What do you want us to do? Take *sanyas* at 35?"

A word of caution to my workaholic friends. It is true that all work is worship of God; and we should put maximum effort into whatever we wish to achieve. But, work should not be killing! It should not drain your spirit or kill you with the slow poison of stress, anxiety and fear. Your work should not cripple you. My dear ones, do not become workaholics, create time for your own self. For, ultimately you have to live for your own self. Allot time for silent meditation, for your soul needs meditation.

A saint invited his disciple, who was a busy official, to come and pray with him during his daily *satsang*.

"I wish I could," said the man. "But the trouble is, Master, I am too busy at the moment!"

"You remind me of a man walking blindfold in the jungle," said the Master. "And he said he was too busy to take the blindfold off."

When the official pleaded lack of time, the Master said, "What a sad mistake it is to think that one cannot pray for lack of time!"

My friends, you find time for everything else. You attend to your business or profession. You make time for family and friends. You set aside time for parties, picnics and movies. How is it that you cannot set aside 15 minutes out of your busy schedule, to sit quietly and commune with God?

Everyone is busy making money nowadays. They think only of millions, and multi-millions. But you cannot take your millions with you, when you leave this world and enter the Great Beyond – as indeed we all must, one day. That day is coming, sure as the sun rises in the east, that day is fast approaching when we will have to leave behind everything – not only all the millions we have made, but also our near and dear ones, family, friends and relatives, our positions, our possessions, our power, all that we have accumulated here. What will we carry with ourselves on that day? What will we take with us when we set out on the inevitable journey of death?

The *satsang* will give you the answers to all these questions.

Very often when we ask people why they are not attending *satsang* regularly, the reply is, "There is no time" or "I am busy with my work" or "I do not even get time to take a deep breath..." and so on. Such excuses cannot fool anyone, not even the people who make these excuses! Some people even say, "Well, when I retire from my active job, I will definitely devote time to *satsang*, spiritual pursuits, and God." But such time rarely comes.

Man's life is so crowded with mundane activities, that he rarely has time for self-study and introspection. He seldom finds himself in that expansive, tranquil mood of silence and reflection, where he can listen to God, and chant the Name Divine in the heart within.

It is said that the worldly desires are like the salty waters of the sea. Such waters can never quench man's thirst. On the contrary, his thirst increases and his craving for fresh water grows even more acute! To drown yourself wholly in this worldly life is akin to quenching your thirst with salt water.

My humble request to all of you, my fellow brothers and sisters, is to spare sometime for *satsang*. By all means do your work sincerely. Work is essential for a human being. It disciplines his mind and exercises his body. Work is a great boon. But we must remember, work is a means, it is not an end. Livelihood must never be confused with life. Do not make your work the objective of your life on this earth. The purpose of your life is to cultivate the soul. Hence, even while you are attending to your work, stay connected to the Source of all Life; stay in constant touch with God. If you are able to set aside personal time, spend some of that valuable time in any form of *sadhana* that appeals to you. If you give eight or nine hours a day to your work, it should not be difficult to spare one or two hours to your spiritual growth! This will help you achieve the kind of inner peace and bliss that work can never bring to you.

Awaken an aspiration in your heart. We read, do we not, that Sri Krishna played tricks with the Gopis, enticed them in his love and then disappeared, leaving the Gopis yearning for him. I hardly need to tell you that this story of Krishna Leela, actually symbolizes the highest aspiration that any human soul can have – that is, the yearning of the *jivatma* (individual soul) for the *paramatma* (the Supreme Being). In the same way, kindle a longing for Him in your heart. Aspiration for the Lord, the burning desire to be in communion with him, will give you the right perspective on worldly wealth and pleasures. *Naam Simran* is not mere chanting, it is a yearning. Let that yearning rise and take you on a higher elevation above the mundane acts of daily living. Let this yearning be a longing – the longing of *Sasui* for *Puno* or *Majnu* for *Laila*. The heart wrenching soulful cry for the Beloved will put you on the spiritual path. You will find He is by you, guiding you at every step of your life.

Very often in the *satsang*, I open my eyes after a meditation or a prayer, and I get the feeling that some of the *satsangis* are present there only physically. Mentally they are elsewhere. Their thoughts wander and take them into worldly worries.

If they would sit in quietude and focus on the *Naam Kirtan*, they could experience many mystical insights. Their physical ailments would disappear. They would taste a rare peace that is born of true inner bliss.

The message of every *satsang* is 'go within'. Go within. Explore your interior world and you will find that Divine Light which dispels every darkness!

When a man falls ill he goes to the hospital to be treated. Even so, when man realises that he is falling a prey to evil, he should go to *satsang*. *Satsang* is like the hospital, which will treat the disease called 'evil'.

A day has twenty four hours and the twenty four hours have fourteen hundred and forty minutes. How much time do you wish to give to God? At least ten percent of the time, that is, two hours and twenty four minutes, you must devote to God. If you are unable to devote two hours and twenty four minutes to God, then keep aside sometime in the morning and sometime in the evening to be spent in *satsang* or in chanting the Name Divine. *Santon Ke Charno Mein Subha Aur Shaam Sunte Rahe Pritam Ka Paigham* – it means, "At the feet of holy ones, morning and evening, may I hear the clarion call of my Beloved."

Who is a true *satsangi*? Not the one who attends the *satsang*, but the one who absorbs the pure vibrations of the *satsang*, listens to every word carefully, goes home and ponders over the teachings and puts them into practice. At times, hundreds of devotees come to *satsang,* but I cannot help thinking that only a handful among them have true spiritual intentions. But, it does not matter. Some of these devotees will surely reap the benefits of the pure and sacred environment, while the others will make a beginning in the right direction.

There was a devotee who had regularly attended *satsang* for 30 years. His son, a young man, often wondered why his father attended the *satsang* everyday. What could he possibly gain out of it? So, one day, he decided to accompany his father and attend the *satsang.* He listened to the discourse about the Creator, who is our Father, our Protector and our Guide. He heard the speaker say, "All Creation is one family. We all are His children and therefore we should help one another." The words touched him deeply, and he carried these words in his heart.

Next day, when he went to open his shop, a cow came along and put her mouth in the sack full of wheat. This young man, having heard the discourse in the *satsang,* was awakened; he realised clearly that all creation is one family and that it was his duty to feed the cow. So he gently patted the cow, as she nibbled the wheat.

When his father saw this, he roundly admonished him, "Can't you see the cow is ruining our grain? Don't just stand there, drive it away!"

The son replied, "How much can the cow eat? 1 Kilo, 2 Kilos or 3 Kilos at most? That will not make us poorer. For God has given us enough."

The father was astonished. He asked his son, "Where did you learn this lesson?" The son replied, "Dear father, I attended the *satsang* yesterday and this was the lesson I learnt there." Hearing this, the father was unhappy. He told his son, "Whatever you hear in *satsang* is only for that moment. Once you are on your job, forget all about it and learn to live a practical life."

That is why I said, a true *satsangi* is the one who carries the message of the *satsang* with him, imbibes it and puts it into practice. You too must be a true *satsangi*.

Gurudev Sadhu Vaswani often used to tell us that there are three kinds of rains. The first one is the pure waters of the *satsang*. These divine waters flow through *shabad kirtan*, through the sacred words of saints and from the scriptures. They flow from the positive circle of the continuous incantation of prayers and *mantras*. These waters of the *satsang* cleanse your interior, and give you an integration of mind, heart and soul. These waters purify you even as the holy waters of the Ganga cleanse you from within. The waters of the *satsang* are indeed a source of great purification.

The very word *satsang,* means fellowship of truth. Truth, as we know, is a hard taskmaster. Truth is ever vigilant and like a sentinel stands brandishing its iron weapon, preventing any unauthorised entry into its domain. For inside the domain of truth, there is only truth, there is One Name, One Shyam, One Ram and One Love. Once you enter this domain you cannot come out. *Satsang* of the true type permits you to glimpse this realm; it enriches, empowers and beautifies the inner self.

The second type of rain is the experience of the interior world. You can contact this source of grace through meditation and silent communion with the Divine, which is offered to you in the *satsang*.

The third type of rain is experienced through selfless service. People go to great extent to 'decorate' or beautify their homes; they spend millions of rupees on buying signature paintings. They spend vast amounts on exotic carpets and rugs, exclusive objects of display, and luxury emulsions to adorn the walls. Millions are spent too, on the exteriors of the houses, designed by architects whose fees alone could provide homes to a dozen homeless people! This kind of extravagance, in a country where 30 million people are said to live below the poverty line, is conspicuous as an indication of our new culture of 'consumption'. There are seriously afflicted people in this country who have no money for their medical treatment, desperate parents who are unable to get their daughters married and in these times of recession, there are many who have lost jobs or are on the verge of losing their jobs and their very livelihood.

How can we, in all conscience, indulge in such personal extravagance amidst all the poverty and misery of our fellow human beings?

We all need to have the experience of selfless service. This is like a shower of blessing and joy that invigorates our very spirits. We should spare at least a part of our expenses to be spent in the service of the poor. The waters of selfless service have a magical effect on the body, mind and spirit. It washes away the 'I' of ego. It washes away the cobwebs of the mind and the lower emotions of the heart. Selfless service washes our inner instrument or *antahkarana*, and leaves us with a lasting feeling of joy that no personal extravagance can ever match!

Selfless service is part of the activities of most spiritual congregations. For beginners, service becomes a happy and easy activity, when undertaken in the company of fellow members of the *satsang*. But we will do well to remember that service should be undertaken with a feeling of devotion. Take it as an opportunity to serve the poor, an opportunity to sublimate yourself, an opportunity to climb one more step towards self growth. Above all do it as an offering to God!

Gurudev Sadhu Vaswani founded the *Sakhi Satsang* in Hyderabad-Sind in 1931, and later, he formed the Brotherhood Association, with the goal of cultivating the soul. The hundreds of brothers and sisters who flocked to join his spiritual gatherings, gradually became regular *satsangis*. To this day, as many of you know, the *satsang* remains the pivot around which all the Mission activities revolve. Everyday, three *satsang* sessions are held on the Mission Campus, and people make it a point not to miss the daily *satsang*. I am told that some of our Sadhu Vaswani Centres overseas, also hold weekly/ bi-weekly/daily *satsangs*, which also attract their own share of regular participants.

A friend once expressed his surprise to me, at the fact that people continue to be drawn to the *satsang*, "in this day and age" as he put it. I responded to his remark with the observation that people needed the *satsang* today, more than their parents and grandparents did in bygone times!

This is not just my personal opinion. Many *satsangis* tell me, that *satsang* gives them a sense of stability, a positive frame of mind, a certain sense of mental well being and peace of mind. They say that *satsang* links them with a Higher energy and in that positive, joyful atmosphere they feel happy and rejuvenated. Whether they hear discourses or recite prayers or read from the *bani* of great ones or participate in singing the Name Divine, they feel elevated. At such times, their minds are free from worldly cares and anxieties; and there awakens a desire within them, the desire to follow in the footsteps of the truly great ones. They yearn to imbibe the ideals of saints and sages, and make their life more meaningful, more worthwhile.

They say, too, that *satsang* cleanses and purifies their thoughts, by its sacred environment and holy vibrations; they are able to discard negative emotions like envy, jealousy, avarice, resentment and anger which trouble all of us at times. In fact, it helps them further by awakening in them the higher impulses that human beings aspire to, such as charity, compassion and philanthropy. And when they yield to these noble impulses, they find that they achieve a sense of harmony and joy that surpasses all worldly satisfaction! In short, they assure me, *satsang* generates a sense of peace and tranquility, which helps them to evolve into a higher state of living and thinking.

Have you heard the beautiful bhajan *'Sukh Sagar Mein Aike, Mat Jao Pyasa Pyare'*? It is one of Gurudev Sadhu Vaswani's immortal compositions. It is a *bhajan* that stirs within us an urge for the higher values of life. The song awakens the slumbering spirit; a sudden realization dawns upon us: My life is precious. Let me make the most of it. Let me not go back from this ocean of grace without tasting its sweet waters. Let me not go back exhausted. But let me drink the Divine Nectar and be blessed with bliss and peace.

This is the time of spiritual awakening, which puts you on the path of self growth. Walking on this path, you feel that you are making your life meaningful and worthwhile; you are happy to walk this path. But, you must know, no path is straight and smooth. It has its share of obstacles, steep gradients, unexpected curves and bends. So too with the path of life. A single trauma can shatter you, and make you feel helpless and ruined. Despair and melancholy constantly seem to wait on you. Troubles and anxieties surround you. At such times, you feel abandoned, your faith becomes vulnerable.

Once, *Rishi* Narada approached Lord Vishnu and requested him humbly: "My Lord! Do tell me about the value and influence of *satsang*. I am eager to know what it can do for the seeker."

Lord Vishnu smiled at Narada. He said, "I am so busy now, I do not have the time to talk to you about it. But I would like to help you. Please go to the giant banyan tree in the forest located at the foot of the Meru Hills. There you will find a squirrel. He will enlighten you about *satsang*."

Rishi Narada was puzzled. A squirrel – to enlighten him on *satsang!* But the Lord's word was absolute, and Narada did as he was told. He found the tree in question, and a lively squirrel jumped down before him.

In all respect, Narada said to him, "I pray you, dear squirrel, enlighten me on the value and influence of *satsang*."

The squirrel looked at Narada with its beady, bright eyes for what seemed to be a long drawn out minute. Narada looked into its eyes and held his gaze. At the end of the minute the squirrel curled up, lifeless. It was dead!

Taken aback, Narada found his way back to *Vaikunth,* where he narrated the moving incident to the Lord. "I hope I have not been instrumental in the death of the poor creature," he lamented. "And, dear Lord, my question is still unanswered. Wilt Thou enlighten me?"

"I'm afraid that's not possible Narada," replied the Lord. "Go back to the same tree. You will find a monkey, who will give you the knowledge you seek."

Faithfully, Narada did as he was told. Indeed, he found the monkey swinging from one branch to another. When he saw Narada, the monkey jumped down with a thud.

"I pray you, O monkey, to enlighten me on the value of *satsang*," Narada said to the monkey respectfully.

The monkey drew close and looked deep into Narada's eyes. In a minute, he dropped dead at the sage's feet.

This time, Narada was nonplussed. In utter shock, he rushed to Lord Vishnu and said: "Lord, I do not know what is wrong. The monkey you mentioned has also dropped dead before my eyes. What am I doing to these poor creatures? Who will now enlighten me on the *satsang?*"

"Well, Narada," said Lord Vishnu. "Tomorrow a prince will be born in the royal family of the kingdom in which the forest is located. Go and bless the new born child – and he will enlighten you on the matter you seek."

"But... my Lord..." stammered Narada. "When I consider the fate of the squirrel... and the monkey... how can I dare to approach this innocent, newborn baby?"

"Do you or don't you need enlightenment on *satsang?*" asked the Lord with a smile. "Go to the child. Your quest will be fulfilled."

It was with a trembling heart that Narada entered the royal palace the next morning. The King and Queen were deeply honoured to see him. They welcomed him with all ceremony that was due to a *maharishi*. They entreated him to bless their newborn son: the heir to the throne.

Narada was taken to the room where the baby prince lay asleep in the cradle. His heart beat fast as he laid his hand on the brow of the child to bless him.

No sooner had he touched the child, than the baby opened its eyes and looked deep into the eyes of the *Rishi*.

"O Prince," said Narada, a cold sweat breaking out over his forehead. "Lord Vishnu bade me come to You to ask You about the value of the *satsang.*"

To the *rishi's* utter amazement, the baby began to speak. "*rishi* Narada, you see me here - the manifest proof of the value of *satsang*. In my previous births, I was a squirrel, and then a monkey. As a squirrel, I was only motivated by appetite. I did nothing but gather and hoard. When I met you and looked into your eyes, I was released from that birth. My *karma* caused me to take birth as a monkey. Then again, I had the good fortune to encounter you at close quarters. Released from that incarnation, I have risen in the scale of evolution to take birth as a Prince in the pious family of the King of this country. If one minute in the company of a holy one like you could help me this far, I leave you to judge what the value and influence of sustained *satsang* can be!"

Narada was overjoyed. The Lord had indeed performed a *leela* to teach his humble devotee the value of *satsang*.

Satsang has a positive effect on man. *Satsang* creates pure and positive vibrations which neutralise the negative emotions of man. When we go to *satsang*, we get to hear discourses of holy men, participate in the recitation of sacred scriptures and singing of soulful *bhajans*. All of this helps to raise the levels of positive vibrations and energises us. For a short time at least, we forget our mundane worries and get immersed in the pure waters of the Spirit. Our emotions rise above the senses, and we cry out, "O Lord! This is bliss. O Lord! You have given me this beautiful gift of life. Till now I have wasted it. But from now onwards, I will strive to achieve the goal of this human birth!"

Unfortunately for us, these emotions of sublimity do not last long. The moment we leave the *satsang*, we are submerged in worldly concerns. We are drawn into the vicious circle of worry, anxiety, envy and jealousy. We are pulled back into the quicksand of pleasures and wrong doing. We are lost in negativity. Dark clouds surround us and we are back where we started. What is the reason? Why could we not sustain those positive energies a little longer? Why is our spiritual effort so short lived?

The reason is simple. Our senses are constantly running after the pleasures of life. But, as the poet John Keats pointed out so perceptively, pleasure and pain are very close to each other: in fact, they are two sides of the same coin.

...and aching Pleasure nigh,

Turning to poison while the bee-mouth sips...

Just consider those phrases; *aching pleasure*, *turning to poison*; even while it is being sipped. Does the poem not say it all? Pleasures bind us, imprison us and ultimately bring us the pain of despair and frustration. Pleasure is poison. Sooner or later, it shows its effect. It destroys man. It kills man.

We live in an uncertain world. The only certainty in this world of uncertainty is that every passing day, every fleeting moment draws us closer to the day when death will come and knock on the door and exclaim, "Vacate the house". The body will then drop down but we shall continue to live in the life that is undying. Are we prepared to face death with courage and equanimity? Have we made the necessary preparations to face our Creator? Have we made ourselves ready for the life after death?

These and other thoughts on similar lines crossed my mind when the mortal remains of a devotee was brought to Gurudev Sadhu Vaswani's sacred *samadhi* for the final prayers. I asked myself, "I know death can come at anytime; but am I prepared for it?"

May I tell you, dear friends, that our life – a little interlude in this world – is part of a Great Design. It is a training ground for self-growth. Very few of us are aware of this purpose. But it is definite that our sojourn on this earth is predestined – perhaps by our own choice – for this life has been given to us for our own spiritual progress and evolution. However, we spend our life in the pursuit of pleasure, thinking that it is the be-all and end-all of our existence. We are so enamoured by the superficial glamour and glitter around us, that we forget the very purpose for which we have come. Daily attendance at the *satsang* will ensure that we do not throw our precious life away in such frivolous pursuits.

People often wonder about what exactly goes on in a *satsang*. What are the disciplines prescribed? What is the message of the discourses? What is the message conveyed through them? So let me tell you a little about the Sadhu Vaswani *satsang*. The discourses in our *satsang* are universal in approach. The main teaching given is this: the gift of the human birth so freely bestowed on all of us is invaluable. Saints and sages of all faiths and all ages have emphasised that human life is God's greatest gift to us. But it is a gift that is meant to fulfil a purpose. It is a rare and valuable gift, and not meant to be wasted on earthly pleasures. It should be used to achieve the ultimate goal – Liberation through service of the Lord, and the suffering children of the Lord.

One of the disciplines we practise in the *satsang* is to sit in silence, meditate and go within the self. For we believe, that in the practise of silence we get answers to the most profound questions that vex our minds. In silence we perceive our true selves.

The practise of silence is not child's play! It is a tough and demanding discipline! Most of you who attempt meditation can vouch for this – the moment we sit in silence to meditate, our mind begins to wander, because the nature of the mind is to wander. It is not only in this birth alone that the mind wanders; it has been wandering through so many births that we have lived earlier. We are born with this restless and roaming mind. That is why, the moment we sit in silence to meditate, all the suppressed thoughts wake up and the mind seems to go berserk, struggling like a frail ship against a rough turbulence.

In the Srimad Bhagavad Gita, Arjuna asks Sri Krishna, "O, Lord, the mind is akin to a storm of lust and desires, and man is carried away by the storm. Is it possible to tame this turbulent mind?" Sri Krishna replies, "O Arjuna, it is true that the mind is like a raging storm. It is difficult to control it, but it is not impossible."

Satsang is nothing but the safest and easiest spiritual routine, that we can give ourselves. It cleanses and purifies our hearts. This cleansing of mind and heart is done through the chanting of the Name Divine, associating with men of God, as well as with like-minded aspirants who share our quest for Liberation, through *kirtan, bhajan* and recitations from the sacred scriptures, as well as listening to discourses that enlighten us. Just as we clean our body with soap and water, similarly we can purify our mind and heart by washing them in the waters of the spirit, the *amrit dhara*, that flows perennially in the *satsang*.

Gurudev Sadhu Vaswani gave us an invaluable message, "Your life on this earth is but a journey, a brief sojourn. Your native home lies beyond this earthly plane; and the passage to the native land is through the *satsang*." The divine presence of a realised soul, a guru, in itself is a boon, for it brings peace and harmony to your soul, just through the spiritual vibrations that his presence generates. *Satsang* offers to you, the flowing waters of the spirit. It enables you to hear the melody of the Name Divine. It cleanses both heart and mind. Therefore, I urge my friends, always join the fellowship of the *satsang* and rejoice in taking dips in the flowing waters of the spirit. Do not ever forsake this beautiful, purifying, blissful experience, that is so freely available to all of us. It is as easy as walking in and taking your seat. The power of the *satsang* will take care of the rest.

A sister once came to see me in a very perturbed state of mind. She said that she had been greatly agitated of late, by a personal crisis that had rocked her life. She needed to talk to me and was anxious for advice. I suggested that as it was nearly time for the evening *satsang,* she should attend the same, and then come to talk to me.

She agreed, and went away to join the *satsang,* which was about to begin. As I remember, it was a Tuesday, which, in our Sadhu Vaswani *satsang,* includes a session of meditation. Every evening when the *satsang* is over, we have a brief session of prayer and silence at Gurudev Sadhu Vaswani's sacred *Samadhi*. After this refreshing and uplifting session, I sent for this sister myself, for she had indeed appeared very disturbed.

She came running up to me and said, "Yes, Dada?"

I gently reminded her that she had wanted to meet me urgently, over a matter that had been troubling her.

"Oh, yes, I remember," she said, with a smile. "But Dada, I really feel I don't need to trouble you and take away your valuable time now. I have found the answer to my questions, the solution to my problem."

She explained that the moment she walked into the *satsang*, she had felt a sense of peace and calm descending on her. As she heard the *kirtan*, she felt unbidden tears flow from her eyes. The day's *vachan* from the *Nuri Granth*, seemed as if it was deliberately addressed to her. She participated in the *aarti*, which she found to be a healing, purifying experience. In the meditation session which followed, she was actually able to hear her inner voice speak to her, and the terrible weight of anxiety and worry that had been pressing down on her, lowering her morale and her spirit, seemed to lift like a cloud. At the end of the session, she literally felt that she was a new person, ready to take on the blows and bullets of life. She had not only received inner guidance to approach her own problem, but was also filled with a sense of well being, courage and confidence. In fact, till I sent for her, she had almost forgotten that she had come to me earlier that evening, in a distraught condition, seeking answers to questions that overwhelmed her. Such was the effect of *satsang* on her!

Indeed, I can vouch for the fact that *satsang* has an abundance of positive energy. We must all avail of it.

We all know that our stay on this earth is temporary. It may be few years or it may be sixty, seventy or even more. But before coming here, where were you? Try and answer this question. Discover for yourself, where is your true home? Unless and until you find an answer to this question, you will continue to wander in this *bazaar* of worldly *maya*.

This wandering is futile, for we have to return to our native land. And the sooner we realize this, the better it is. *Satsang* is the easy passage to that true abode. Hence, *satsang* is very important for everyone of us.

All the religions of the world, in some way or the other, refer to the native land/home. Two thousand years ago, Sri Isha (Jesus), came to this earth to awaken the slumbering. "Awake, stand up and let's walk to the Kingdom of God," he said. Those who yearn to see the Beauteous face of the Lord, should know that the gate which opens to the kingdom of God is small, narrow and straight.

Says Sant Kabir, "Find a man of God who can open the door so that you can pass through easily."

I have often reflected on these words. He says too, as we saw earlier, that the door to the ultimate freedom (*mukti*) is very, very small. It is as small as the eye of a needle. To enter you have to be as small as a point. The *satsang* and the *satpurkha* who conducts the *satsang* will teach and train us how to be so. That is why we should build a strong and timeless bond with *satsang*. In the *satsang*, we get associated with a man of God and he blesses us with spiritual treasures. Truly speaking, triple is the treasure that one receives from a man of God. However we should go to a *satsang* with a yearning and a thirst for spiritual knowledge. The yearning should be deep, as deep as when floundering in the darkness, one yearns for a ray of light. Go to *satsang* with devotion, with love, with yearning and you will receive the triple treasure of spirituality.

What are these three treasures that we receive from *satsang?*

The first treasure is that we learn meditation. Sitting at the lotus feet of a holy one, we learn to meditate. Meditation stills our restless mind. The treasure of meditation / concentration is found only by those *satsangis* who go there with true devotion. It is said, "Through concentration, you will experience bliss." First we learn concentration. And then we move to meditation, which takes us to the higher regions of awareness and bliss!

The second treasure which we receive is *naam kirtan* / chanting the Name Divine. By chanting the Name Divine, by immersing ourselves into the holy waters of the spirit, we are relieved of many tensions. By chanting the Name Divine, our *antah-karan* – inner instrument gets purified; it draws our senses to a focus, and we feel refreshed.

The third treasure which we receive from *satsang* is prayer. What is prayer? Prayer is contact with the Unseen. It is the link to the Universal Self. Prayer helps us to build a relationship with the Invisible. Prayer is a rare treasure and he who knows to pray is truly blessed.

How can we gather to ourselves the true treasure of *satsang*? So let me give you a few practical suggestions:

1. Seek the company of people who go to the *satsang*. Association with them will give you the impulse to enter the world of the *satsang*, a world of spiritual quietude and prayer.

2. Set apart some time everyday to refrain from worldly activities and focus on the inner world within you. Enter into nurturing activities like meditation, recitation from the scriptures, etc.

3. Keep yourself away from all unproductive talk, gossip and controversies. Do not criticize others, nor entertain gossip about them.

4. Do not miss your daily appointment with God. Fix a time for your meditation. Resolve that you will meditate for 15 minutes or half an hour or an hour. During this period you can chant the Name Divine, you can commune with God, meditate on some inspirational teachings, or pick

up a sentence from a spiritual literature on compassion, oneness, etc. and reflect on it.

This world is a travellers' Inn. People come here, stay for a while and then return to where they came from. We are only short-term guests here upon earth. But we have our responsibilities, even as guests and visitors. While we are staying at the travellers' Inn, we have to be very cautious and take care of our most valuable belongings. We have to be wakeful.

The other day, a fellow devotee told me of his sad plight. He was travelling to Pune by train. He fell asleep for a while. When he woke up and got down at the railway station, he discovered that he had been robbed of his wallet. He had lost all his money and the railway ticket. Just imagine what happens when a traveller falls asleep for a while and loses his valuables.

My dear brothers and sisters, do not fall into slumber while you are a visitor upon this earth. If you are not wakeful, you may lose all your valuable belongings.

Living in the world as we do, our minds cannot remain steady without the protecting influence of *satsang* – fellowship with the pure and holy.

Saints and sages, *rishis* and holy men have shown us many paths leading to happiness. But the path which is open to each one of us is very easy and it is the path of *satsang* –

fellowship. *Satsang* does not mean passivity; it does not mean just being physically present in the *satsang* hall. *Satsang* means true fellowship with everyone. True *satsang* means being immersed in *bhakti*. True *satsang* means love for all. True *satsang* means earning the blessings by being His instrument of service to others. When you go to *satsang* you earn your own reward: you imbibe the teachings imparted by the holy ones; you ponder over the sacred words of the scriptures; you internalise the spiritual values taught in the *satsang* and you automatically begin to make the effort to bear witness to the teachings of the great ones in your daily life.

May the holy men and women of God shower their benedictions on us! May we build our lives in prayer and faith. May we learn to open the door that shows us the passage to our Native land! May we move out of darkness into that wonderful sphere of light!

• • • • • • • •

The hands that help are holier than those
that turn the beads of the rosary.

J. P. Vaswani

• • • • • • • •

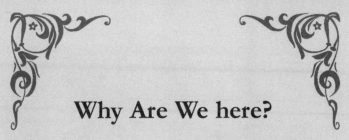

Why Are We here?

There was a little boy who asked his mother, "Mom, why are we here upon this earth?"

"To help others, my son!" replied the mother instantly.

"Then, what are the others here for?" retorted the boy.

Very often, we begin to discriminate about *whom* we should help, and who deserves our help more than others.

Long ago, I received a book called *The Greatest Is Love*, in which the story is told of a lawyer who prided himself on being an outstanding scholar on the Laws of Moses. He met Jesus and asked to have a discussion on what a man should do to live forever in heaven.

"You are the expert on the subject," smiled the Lord. "You tell me, what does Moses' law say about it?"

"It says," the lawyer replied, clearing his throat peremptorily, "It says that you must love the Lord with all your heart, all your strength, all your soul and all your mind."

"Is that all?" asked the Lord.

"Well, it says that you must love your neighbour just as much as you love yourself."

"Right," said the Lord. "So that is all you have to do in order to dwell forever in Heaven."

Now the lawyer certainly did not love his neighbours as he loved himself. He wanted to argue this point with the Lord – that one could not love *all* one's neighbours.

"Now this is not clear or specific," he argued. "For instance, I have so many neighbours. Which of them should I love?"

By way of answer, Jesus narrated to him the parable of the good Samaritan.

A Jew was on his way from Jerusalem to Jericho. He was accosted by a band of robbers who beat him up, stripped him, robbed him of all that he carried with him and left him half dead by the road side.

A Jewish priest who passed by the spot a little later, saw the man and hastily crossed over to the other side of the road, averting his eyes. A Jewish temple assistant came along, cast a curious glance at the unconscious form of the man, and walked on.

Then a despised Samaritan came along. He was moved to pity at the sight of the wounded man. He knelt by the man's side, cleaned his wounds and bandaged them. He covered the naked man with a blanket, put him on his donkey and took him to the nearest inn, where he nursed him throughout the night.

Next morning, he paid the innkeeper a considerable sum of money to lodge the wounded man and care for him till he came back from his journey. "I will pay all the money you need," the Samaritan assured him sincerely.

"Who do you think proved to be a true neighbour for the victim?" the Lord asked the lawyer.

"The one who took pity on him," murmured the lawyer.

"That is what you must do too," the Lord said to him.

THE SEVENTH GATEWAY TO HEAVEN:
SERVICE

Let me begin this chapter with the inspiring words of India's national poet, Rabindranath Tagore:

This is my prayer to thee, my Lord – strike, strike at the root of penury in my heart.
Give me the strength lightly to bear my joys and sorrows.
Give me the strength to make my love fruitful in service.
Give me the strength never to disown the poor.
Or bend my knees before insolent might.
Give me the strength to raise my mind high above daily trifles.
And give me the strength to surrender my strength to Thy Will with love.

Gurudev Sadhu Vaswani, was once asked, "What is your religion?" His reply was truly significant. He said, "I know of no religion higher than the religion of unity and love, of service and sacrifice."

For him, indeed, to live was to serve, to live was to love, to live was to bear the burdens of others, to live was to share his all with all.

One evening, as we were taking a walk on the roadside with Gurudev Sadhu Vaswani we saw a poor man lying underneath a tree. His clothes were tattered and torn; his feet were covered with mud. Gurudev Sadhu Vaswani stopped at the sight of this man. He asked for a bucket of water to be brought. And when it was brought, this prince among men – he had but to lift up a finger and hundreds of us would rush to find out what his wish was – with his own hands he cleansed the body of the poor beggar and passed on to him his own shirt to wear! The poor man pointed to the cap on Gurudev Sadhu Vaswani's head, and without the least hesitation, the Master passed on the cap to him. On that occasion he spoke certain words, which I can never, ever forget. He said, "This shirt and this cap and everything that I have, is a loan given to me to be passed on to those whose need is greater than mine."

> **May I become at all times,**
> **both now and forever,**
> **A protector for those**
> **without protection,**
> **A guide for those who**
> **have lost their way**
> **A ship for those with oceans to cross**
> **A bridge for those with rivers to cross**
> **A sanctuary for those in danger**
> **A lamp for those without light**
> **A place of refuge for those**
> **who lack shelter**
> **And a servant to all in need.**
> *–Buddhist Prayer*

Mark the word *loan* – everything that we have is a loan given to us, to be passed on to those whose need is greater than ours. Nothing belongs to us; nothing has been given to us absolutely; everything has been given to us as a loan – our time and our talents, our knowledge, our experience, our wisdom, our prestige, our influence in society, our bank accounts, our property and possessions, our life itself is a loan given to us to be passed on to those whose need is greater than ours. In these simple words of the Master, as it seems to me, are enshrined the seeds of a new humanity, a new world order, a new civilization of service and sacrifice.

The following *subhashita* (gem of speech) is attributed to Sage Ved Vyasa:

> All the wisdom that is taught through innumerable books may be summed up, in half-a-verse, thus: "To serve humanity is meritorious, and to harm anyone is sinful."

Service, it has been rightly said, is the rent we have to pay for being tenants of this body. Every morning, as we wake up, we must ask ourselves this question: What can I do to help? What can I do to make a difference? For indeed, each one of us can and must make a difference. There are so many tasks to be accomplished by us: there are hungry ones to be fed; there are naked ones to be clothed; there are elders to be cared for; there are children to be taught. There is so much work to be done! And every one of us – from the youngest to the oldest – can make a difference.

There is not much that I can do on my own," is what many of us think. We are mistaken. The tragedy for many of us is not that our aim is too high and we miss it – but rather that our aim is too low and we reach it!

As Herschel Hobbs says, "The world measures a man's greatness by the number who serve him. Heaven's yardstick measures a man by the number who are served by him."

Indeed, it is this caring spirit that we all need. When I go to big cities like Mumbai, Delhi, Kolkatta and Chennai, I find that people seem to have stopped caring. They have become insensitive, indifferent to the needs of those around them. Their attitude to the suffering and misery they see around them is defined by the words: "It's none of our business."

Surely, it's our business! Mankind is our business. The Vedas give us the wonderful concept of *Vasudaiva Kutumbakam*. Humanity is one family; and in this one family of humanity, every man is my brother; every woman is my sister. It is my duty, to do all I can to help them to the best of my ability, to the best of my capacity. I must do all I can, to help as many as I can, in as many ways as I can, to lift the load on the rough road of life. I often say to people: the opposite of love is not hatred; the opposite of love is apathy – indifference to the needs of those around us.

We are all born with the spirit of caring and sharing. But somewhere along the way, as we grow older, we lose this wonderful spirit. Children care – and they always show that they care.

I read a beautiful story about an elementary school in Chicago, where the children got together to put up a Christmas pageant. A third grader was to play the role of the inn–keeper. He had but one line of dialogue to deliver: "Sorry, there is no room at this inn."

> **Send Thy peace, O Lord,**
> **our Father and Mother**
> **That we, thy children on Earth,**
> **May all unite in one family.**
> *–Islamic Prayer*

However, the spirit of Christmas entered into this little boy, and he played his part with real feeling. "Sorry," he said to Mary and Joseph, "there is no room at this inn." But as they turned away, the little fellow called out, "Come back, Joseph, come back! I will give you my room!" Perhaps this is why Jesus told his disciples to become like little children!

A great man was asked, "What are the three most important things in the life of a human being?" He answered, "The first is to care, the second is to care, the third is to care."

The Chinese have a number of proverbs and aphorisms, rich in the wisdom of life. One of these proverbs tells us: "If you want to be happy for an hour, take a nap. If you want to be happy for a day, go out for a picnic. If you want to be happy for a month, get married. If you want to be happy for a year, inherit a fortune. And if you want to be happy for a lifetime, go out and serve others."

Serve others – for life is too short; so let us be quick to love and prompt to serve. The day on which you have not served someone in need, a brother here, a sister there, a bird here, an animal there – the day on which you have not served a fellow being is a lost day indeed!

A lot of us tend to believe that the little that we can do, counts for nothing, against the vast canvas of the world's misery and suffering. But just as little drops of water together make the mighty ocean, so too, little acts of kindness and compassion can and will make a difference.

When we start living and working for others, then our lives too, become richer, more rewarding, more meaningful. We are able to tap our inner *shakti* to its highest potential; we become more energetic; we become more creative; we solve problems easily. Above all, we grow in the consciousness that all life is One, all life is sacred, all men are brothers – and that birds and animals too, are our brothers and sisters in the One family of Creation. Is not this the highest form of consciousness – this awareness of the Unity of all life?

We all start off by doing our duty towards our family, our profession, our near and dear ones. This purifies our inner instrument. But we should not stop there. We must grow in the awareness that we do not belong merely to our immediate family, we belong to a larger family – to the community, to the society, to the nation, to humanity at large, to creation in all its variety and splendour!

One day, a man came to meet my Beloved Master, Sadhu Vaswani. There was a gleam in his eye, a smile on his lips, vigour in his step as he eagerly greeted the Master and said, "Bless me Master, for today has been a lucky day, a happy day, a wonderful day for me!"

Gurudev Sadhu Vaswani asked him, "What has happened today?"

The man replied, "Today, I have signed a contract worth ten lakhs – in a single day, I have earned a profit of three lakhs!"

Let me tell you that in those days, three lakhs would have been the equivalent of three crores today! In those days people hardly spoke of crores or millions. A lakh was a lot of money!

The Master looked at this man lovingly, and asked him in a very soft and gentle voice "Did you feed a poor man today? Did you offer water to a thirsty one? Did you offer a piece a cloth to a naked one? Did you utter a word of comfort to someone in distress?"

The man was taken aback. "No Dada," he confessed honestly. "I haven't done any of these things." He added after a little thought, "It didn't even occur to me to do any of those things."

Then Gurudev Sadhu Vaswani said to him, "How can this be your lucky day, a wonderful, happy day? Your day has been wasted if you have not helped someone in need!"

Alas, we keep on wasting day after day if we neglect the opportunity to save others, to bring comfort to the depressed, to help the poor and the underprivileged, to bring joy in to the lives of joyless ones.

> **Do all the good you can, by all the means you can, in all the ways you can, in all the places you can, at all the times you can, to all the people you can and as long as you can.**
> —*John Wesley*

This should be the mark of our daily schedule – to do our duty and a little more!

Let service be a part of our larger duty. Unless we go out of ourselves, we can never be truly happy.

Look around you, and you will find the world is sad, torn by tragedy and smitten with suffering. Living in such a world we must share with others, whatever God has given to us in

His infinite mercy. It has rightly been said that service is a debt, the rent that we have to pay for inhabiting the human body. It is a debt, the rent we have to pay for the many favours that we have received from God and the surrounding Universe. We can pay off this debt only by serving those less fortunate than ourselves – the poor, the needy, the disabled, the old and the orphaned ones.

The ancient legends tell us of a great and noble King who devoted his life to the service of his people. His every moment, every breath, every effort was spent towards working for the welfare of his people.

> **This is the sum of all true righteousness — treat others as thou wouldst thyself be treated. Do nothing to thy neighbour, which hereafter, thou wouldst not have thy neighbour do to thee.**
> **A man obtains a proper rule of action by looking on his neighbour as himself.**
> *—Hinduism*

When the call of death came to this King, whom the people loved and revered as a saint, an angel of God came to escort him to heaven, which he had earned as his right, with his good deeds.

To the angel, the King, made an unusual request: "May I be permitted to visit hell before I enter the Kingdom of Heaven?"

Perhaps the angel was a little surprised by this request! However he consented graciously, promising to take the King to hell, as well as to be with him as an escort during the visit.

The King went to hell, accompanied by the angel. But he was amazed by the sight that met his eyes. Happy faces surrounded him. People were delighted to see him; they greeted him with great joy. There was rejoicing and contentment wherever he turned.

"Surely, this is not hell!" he whispered to the angel. "You have brought me to Heaven directly."

"No, Your Majesty," said the angel. "This is indeed the other place."

"But..." protested the King, "I had always imagined hell to be a place of terrible pain and suffering! This place radiates joy and contentment."

"Alas, this place is full of pain and suffering, though you may not see it before you. Everywhere else, where you cannot see, people groan in misery. But being in your holy presence has brought peace and joy to these people."

"If that is so, I have found my heaven right here," said the King. "This is where I shall stay. For what is greater than bringing joy to the joyless ones?"

There are terrible problems confronting the world today – starvation, poverty, war, violence, religious fanaticism, environmental degradation and more! It is enough to depress the most optimistic among us. And so, even the best of us exclaim in despair: "What can we do? How much can we do? What ever we do, it's not going to be enough!"

True: it may not be enough, but that should be no reason for us to desist from all action. Rather, we must do what we can, in the firm faith and belief, "I *can* make a difference! I *will* make a difference."

If all of us worked in this spirit, the world will surely be a better place!

Many people in India, when they are urged to be selfless, honest, loving and forgiving, and take to a life of service and sacrifice, retort angrily, "I am not Mahatma Gandhi!"

Too true, we are not Mahatmas. But then Gandhiji was not transformed into a Mahatma overnight. He had to struggle; he had to confront failure and hardship; he was even kicked and beaten in South Africa, before he decided to devote his life to the service of the downtrodden, the deprived and the oppressed of the world.

> **Dost thou know who is the rejector of faith? The one who neglects the orphan; and never advocates the feeding of the poor... Ye shall be charitable, for Allah loves the charitable.**
> *–The Qur'an*

Many were the people who had to face the same failure and ill treatment before Gandhi. Why, thousands of Indians must have been victims of the inhuman apartheid regime in South Africa before he even set foot in that country. But these bitter, harsh experiences transformed a young, struggling, lawyer into a 'great soul' determined to fight against all forms of oppressions and injustice. He went to South Africa to earn a living; he learnt the most valuable lesson of his life – that one had to live and fight for others – not just for oneself alone.

Selfless service is the bridge that will take you from the life of the world to the life of the spirit.

Andrew Carnegie was a famous industrialist of the USA. He was a great man. He was born in Scotland, immigrated to the USA. He began his career by doing odd jobs and with luck and hard work he became one of the wealthiest men in America. He was a steel magnate. Andrew Carnegie earned millions of dollars. One day he asked himself, what will I do with so much money? He therefore adopted a rule for himself that he will carry home only that much which would give him a comfortable living. All the profits earned over and above would go into charity. He put a limit to his expenditure. Subsequently, with the extra money he set up the Andrew Carnegie Foundation. The Foundation was created to open schools, colleges, hospitals, museums and research laboratories. The Foundation generated employment, it contributed to social upgradation. It helped in the development of deprived areas. All this was possible because of just one man. He said, "When you die rich, you die disgraced."

We should imbibe this lesson and donate all the money over and above that which is required for our comfortable living. We should donate money in charity and towards selfless service. Selfless service is also an instrument of self growth and self evolution. Through service of mankind we can wipe away much of our bad *karma*.

We save money for the future of our children. We save money for the security of our future. But there should be a limit to this. How much can you leave for your children? Too much money and too much luxury will only spoil the children. Let children learn to be self dependent. Let them learn the value of money. Take care of them, provide security for them, but at the same time spare some of your wealth, give away some money in the service of mankind.

Gurudev Sadhu Vaswani would often tell us, "I have but one tongue. If I had a million tongues, I would still utter the one word – give, give, give!"

Give, give, give! Give today, give now, for tomorrow may be too late! If you keep postponing your good intentions for the morrow, and if death overtakes you, you will have to leave behind all the wealth you have accumulated. Man cannot carry anything with him beyond death. He must enter the heaven–world empty handed, for there are no systems to issue travellers' cheques in that world! And no one in heaven is going to be impressed by what you have left behind. You will be asked instead, what you have brought with you to this 'other' world. In the heavenly world, the material wealth accumulated during your earthly sojourn does not count. It is the wealth of good deeds which will accompany you on the inevitable journey. Hence, my dear brothers and sisters, earn the true treasure of the spirit, accumulate the wealth of good deeds, of kind and compassionate service for the world beyond. Every day, give something in charity; give alms with your own hands. Do good deeds, earn true grace, and be richly blessed.

I am amazed at how people are led by their insatiable desires. I was once invited to a house–warming gathering. The owner of the house showed me the expensive fitted furniture that he had specially ordered for the new house. But it seemed to me that his happiness was tinged with anxiety and fear for the future. "I am afraid I have exceeded the budget that I set for myself," he said to me in private. "It will be a tough job to repay the mortgage on this house. I shall not be in peace till I have paid off the housing loan."

Furniture, curtains, modular kitchens, fitted bathrooms and expensive carpets are not enough to make a man happy. Happiness comes from within and not from external trappings, and expensive possessions. If we want to be happy, we should opt out of this mad race for material possessions. We should reduce our wants and control our desires. Therefore, Gurudev Sadhu Vaswani said to us, again and again: Follow the little way, the humble way, the way of service. Live for others and not for self.

Whatever work you do, do it as an offering to the Master. This will help you to be honest and sincere in your work. You will work without any expectation. You will accept work as an opportunity for service to the Lord.

A few days ago, some of our *satsangis* were sent out to go and distribute their own share of a meal among the poor people. They came back to tell us that they had a wonderful experience. One of them said, "I gave my meal to a visually impaired man and I felt as if I was giving food to Gurudev Sadhu Vaswani. I felt immense joy within. The experience was uplifting and fulfilling. The blind man was also happy to receive food. His face glowed with happiness."

Service to other people, especially to the underprivileged can be a truly inspiring and uplifting experience, a source of real joy. My only wish is that more and more of us should taste the nectar of this joy!

The gift of the human birth, so freely bestowed on us, is invaluable. Saints and sages of all faiths and all ages have emphasised that human life is God's greatest gift to us. But it is a gift that is meant to fulfill a purpose. It is a rare and valuable gift, and not meant to be wasted on earthly pleasures. It should be used to achieve the ultimate goal – Liberation through service.

Of course we must continue to work in the world. We must continue in all our struggles and efforts. For, this entire world is a training ground. It is a *yagna*, where we have to put in our bit of sacrifice. God has created the world, and the Universe bears witness to cosmic sacrifice. The Creator has created you in this cosmic sacrifice; and you too have to offer your share of the sacrifice and give the world a bit of yourself.

If you are afraid of the word 'sacrifice', let me assure you that God does not demand great things of us. He wants us to walk the little way. All He asks is this: that you do your duty, offer your service, with devotion and dedication. God is pleased with little things. Small prayers, small sacrifices, little charity, a little service; a little prayer and devotion pleases God, if it is offered in a spirit of reverence and dedication.

A man had the ambition to become a member of Parliament. With this intention, he began to 'serve' the community. It would be truer to say that he was 'cultivating' his future constituency – for his service was being offered with a selfish motive, to get people's votes and get elected in the forthcoming elections. Such selfishness can never give us the joy of true service. Selfish intentions only lead to restlessness, whereas selfless and altruistic service to society brings its own special satisfaction and reward.

But to get back to my story about this ambitious politician: as we know, there is no end to man's ambition and greed. As he continued his 'service' to get himself elected, he was not very pleased when he saw others offering similar 'service' to the people. He made great efforts to undermine others' efforts. What if the people lost out on benefits to their locality in the bargain? After all, he was not really in the business of helping others; he only wanted to help himself. And he would brook no competition even in doing good to others. This is how good deeds get vitiated, when our intentions are not pure!

Soon, our man became an MP, but his ambition soared still higher. He wanted to become a state minister and then, eventually, the chief minister. The nature of worldly desires is such, is it not? The more you get, the more you want. This man was just a self–server. He did not even know the meaning of true service.

Once, Mother Teresa was being interviewed for BBC Television. The interviewer remarked that in a way, the life of dedicated service might be much easier for her than for ordinary householders.

After all, he pointed out, she had no possessions, no insurance, no car, and no husband to care for!

Mother Teresa smiled and said to him, "I'm married too!" She held up the ring that nuns of the Order of the Sisters of Charity wear, to symbolize their "marriage" to Christ. She added, "He can be very difficult at times!"

It takes courage to serve with love!

Survivors of the 9/11 World Trade Centre tragedy tell us that as the twin towers began to burn, they saw the following acts of courage, compassion, loving kindness and selfless service:

- One man slowly lowered a physically disabled colleague in a wheel chair, and took him down carefully, one step at a time, down sixty–eight floors, while all around them, people were rushing down, nearly mad with fear of losing their lives. The man in the wheel chair and his compassionate colleague got out in time.

- Yet another man stood at the landing outside his office, handing out wet paper towels to use as smoke masks to hundreds of people who descended before him.

- As panic stricken office workers poured out of the twin towers, teams of firemen and police rushed in fearlessly, motivated by their strong sense of duty and loving compassion.

- True, there is suffering all around us. But wherever there is suffering, there are also fearless, courageous, compassionate people who take on the sorrows of others as their own. They help others without hesitation; they serve selflessly; they care, they help, they heal!

Many of us are told, when we are little children, that heaven and hell are "places" that we will go to after our death. Indeed, many of us continue to believe, even as adults, that we will be transported to these "places" when we die. But saints and sages tell us that heaven and hell are states of consciousness, conditions of the mind. Even while we live on this earth, we can live in a hell or heaven of our own making.

There was a man who often thought of life after death. One night, he dreamt a strange dream in which he had a vision of hell and heaven.

First, he dreamt that he visited hell. He was astonished to find thousands of people there, with a delicious banquet spread out before them. Every tasty dish, every gourmet delicacy that you and I could dream of, was laid out in that astonishing spread he beheld in "hell".

But to his amazement, he saw that the occupants of hell were thin, emaciated and starving! Not a morsel of the delicious food could they lift and put into their mouths! They stared longingly at the veritable feast spread out before them; they even lifted a morsel or two – but try as they might, they could not take it into their mouths to feed themselves.

Looking closely, the man saw something peculiar – every one of the occupants of hell had arms which were straight as rods. Their arms could not be bent. And so it was that though they could touch the food and even pick it up in their hands, they could not bend their arms and reach it to their mouths.

The man saw this, and was shocked! Little had he imagined that hell would be such!

Next, he visited the heaven world in his dream. A very familiar sight greeted him there, too. All the people had straight arms, which could not be bent; and the same delicious feast was laid out before them.

"But what is the difference between heaven and hell?" asked the man in astonishment.

"Look closely," said an angel who happened to pass by.

It was then that the man saw that the occupants of heaven were happy, smiling, cheerful and blooming with good health. They picked up the morsels of the delicious food and fed it to their friends around them. True, their arms could not be bent, but they could easily reach across to the others around them. True, no one could feed himself – but the people around him took good care to see that he was fed. No one was feeding himself; everyone was feeding another.

"Nothing for myself, everything for others." If this were the motto of your life, you would surely live in heaven on earth!

It was Albert Einstein who said, "Only a life lived for others is worth living." We can also add, "Only a life of giving and sharing is worth living."

Swami Vivekananda put forward the highest concept of service when he coined the term *Daridra Narayana* – the Lord in the form of the poor – and asked people to serve Him. "Where would you go to seek God?" he asked. "Are not all the poor, the miserable, the weak gods? Why not worship them first?"

Swamiji had the compassionate heart of a mother. When a famine was raging in Bengal and his followers could not get money to carry out relief work, he seriously thought of selling the Belur Math property, which he had just purchased to set up the spiritual centre of the Ramakrishna Mission.

So intense was his compassion, so noble his spirit of service that he once said to a friend, "The thought comes to me that even if I have to undergo a thousand births to relieve the misery of the world, aye, even to remove the least pain from anyone, I shall cheerfully do it. Of what use is my personal *mukti* alone? I shall take everyone along that path with myself!"

An ancient legend tells us that someone asked Sri Krishna, "Tell us Lord, which is your favourite name among the thousand names by which we call You?"

The Lord replied, "It is *Deenabandhu* — friend of the weak and the oppressed. That is the name I love best."

The Bhagavad Gita imposes on the devout believer, the duty of *yajna* or sacrifice. Mahatma Gandhi interprets sacrifice to mean service. He points out that the Gita also tells us: "He who cooks only for himself is a thief." There is no higher law than the law of *yajna*, the law of service. "True *yajna* is an act directed to the welfare of others, done without desiring any returns for it, whether of a temporal or spiritual nature," Gandhiji says. "This body therefore, has been given to us only so that we may serve all creation with it."

My beloved Master, Sadhu Vaswani was indeed a great soul, who was "Born To Serve". Everyday, Gurudev Sadhu Vaswani sat underneath the trees he loved, and gave to the poor and broken ones who came to him. He gave them money, he gave them food, he gave them clothing. Above all, he gave them the benedictions of his loving heart.

Literally, till the last day of his earth–pilgrimage, he served the poor and broken ones. In their faces he beheld the Face of God. Every human being, every creature, was to him an image of the King of Beauty. To bring joy into the lives of the starving, struggling, sorrowing ones was one of the deepest aspirations of his life.

A man came to him, one day, and giving him a bundle of notes said, "Gurudev! Here is some money for your temple." What did he do? He utilised the amount in feeding the poor, saying, "The noblest temple is the heart of a poor man, who gets his food and who blesses the Name of God!"

Gurudev Sadhu Vaswani never longed for the joys of the heaven–world. He did not aspire to *mukti*, salvation, liberation from the cycle of birth and death.

The question was put to him more than once, "Is there anything higher than *mukti*?"

He answered, "I do not ask for *mukti*. I fain would be born, again and again, if only that I might be of some help to those that suffer and are in pain!"

Does not the Sri Krishna tell us, "Whatever you give to the least of men, you give unto me?" We will do well to remember that the Lord lives in the lowly and the humble. When we serve them, we serve Him. So it was that Gurudev Sadhu Vaswani said, "Service of the poor is worship of the Lord."

Gurudev Sadhu Vaswani also said, "If you would be happy, make others happy." These beautiful words are carved on the pedestal of his statue, which greets everyone who enters the city of Pune, at the Sadhu Vaswani Chowk, where the Pune cantonment meets Pune city.

Do you wish to be happy? Then make others happy!

Truer words were never spoken. For the happiness that goes out of you to others, comes back to you. Such is the law! Therefore, I tell everyone I meet, do at least one good deed of service everyday.

Gurudev Sadhu Vaswani often said to us:

> Did you see him on the road? Did you leave him with the load?

On the road of life are many who carry loads on their weak shoulders: and the loads are not merely physical. As you bear the loads of others, you will find that your heart is filled with a wondrous feeling of happiness and joy.

"No man is an island," wrote the poet John Donne. The "others" as we think of them are not apart from us. We and others are parts of the One Great Whole. We must not cut ourselves off from others. If we wish to live a healthy, happy life – mentally, morally, spiritually – we must be concerned about the welfare of others, specially our less fortunate brothers and sisters. The selfish man, who is interested only in his own welfare and that of his near and dear ones, is never a happy man. It is only when we go out and make others happy, that happiness flows into our own lives.

The Jewish Talmud tells us the story of a man who had three friends: two of them he loved dearly, but the other, he did not esteem very highly.

One day, the man received summons to appear at the king's court of justice. Greatly alarmed by the summons, he anxiously entreated his two best friends to go with him and plead his cause.

The first one flatly refused to accompany him. The second one relented and agreed to accompany him – but only as far as the gates of the court, and no farther.

Stunned by their refusal, the man reluctantly turned to the friend whom he least esteemed. To his surprise, this friend not only agreed to go all the way with him, but also pleaded his case so effectively before the king, that the man was acquitted.

This same Talmudic story has been rewritten as an old English morality play called *Everyman*. Everyman is summoned by

Death to appear before God. The 'friend' whom he loves most of all, his worldly wealth, cannot go with him even for a single step of the way. His second 'friend', his family and his relatives, can only accompany him to the graveside, but cannot defend him before the Divine Judge. It is his third 'friend', whom he does not esteem highly – his GOOD DEEDS – who goes with him right up to the seat of Justice, and speaks for him and wins his acquittal!

Wealth does not count; words do not count; actions count! Selfless deeds of service count most of all! "Let not my lips but my life speak!"

Mother Teresa, did exactly that; she served the homeless, the destitute, the dying, the forsaken and forlorn – she called them the unwanted and the unloved – with utter love and devotion. She made selfless service the mission and the message of her life. She gathered to her heart those who had been rejected by the cruel world. She came to be known as 'The Saint of the Gutters'.

Accepting the Nobel Peace Prize, Mother Teresa observed quite simply, that when we reach the end of our earthly pilgrimage, we will not be judged by our degrees and diplomas, or by the wealth we have accumulated. Only one thing would matter then: the service that we have rendered to those who need it most; the care and compassion we have offered to the unwanted and unloved.

How may we cultivate the spirit of selfless service? Let me offer you a few practical suggestions:

1. Serve Silently

The very first rule of service is: Serve Silently! Do not serve for show or publicity. Let the right hand not know what your left hand gives away.

I am afraid that today, we serve with cries and clamour. We seem to have confounded service with show and noise. There are so many people who do a little act of service, and spend a sleepless night, only to get up anxiously in the morning and scan the newspapers eagerly to see if their little act of service has been reported in the press!

There was a man who announced that he would be distributing tins of milk powder among slum-dwellers. The poor people – old men, women and children—were invited to come and stand in rows. The milk-powder tins were brought out, and the poor people waited eagerly to receive them – but the man would not begin the distribution. Fifteen minutes passed, half an hour passed; one hour passed. The slum–dwellers grew restless. "Why aren't we getting the milk powder as promised?" they wanted to know.

The answer they got made no sense to them: because the photographer had not arrived!

The "generous donor" was anxious to have his photograph taken in the act of distributing the milk powder. Until the photographer arrived he could not switch on his generosity.

This, my friends, is not true service! I am sometimes deeply saddened when I think of the shadows we run after – name, fame, greatness, popularity and publicity. The true strength of a nation is not in popularity and publicity – the true strength of a country, the true strength of a community, the true strength of a society is in those who serve silently!

2. Serve Humbly

The second principle of service is: Serve Humbly!

Serve with humility – and this is no easy task. Many of us are apt to imagine that the act of giving – of our time, money, effort or resources – is an act of superiority. We feel that we are conferring a great favour – doing *meherbani*, as they say in Hindi – on those whom we seek to serve. I think, it should be the other way round. We should be grateful to those who give us the opportunity to be of service to them.

We have received countless blessings from God. We are in receipt of so many favours from the marvellous universe we live in. We owe a debt of gratitude for these innumerable blessings conferred upon us. This debt we will be able to pay back only if we go out and serve the less fortunate ones: the aged, the infirm, the handicapped, the halt, the unwanted, the unloved, the hopeless and the homeless ones. We should be deeply grateful to them, for they are giving us the opportunity to serve them – and so, to give back at least a fraction of all that we have received from the Lord.

Let us serve humbly – therefore, let us seek no reward for our service – not even a simple words of thanks. For expectation of any return, in any form, makes our service conditional.

We knew a man who had served society for years together. One day he came to meet Gurudev Sadhu Vaswani and said to him, "You know how I have served the people all these years. Now I want them to vote for me and elect me to the Loksabha."

Gurudev Sadhu Vaswani smiled and said to him, "My friend, the reward of service is more service!"

Let us strive to serve humbly – let us seek no reward for our service!

3. Serve lovingly

The third rule of service is: Serve Lovingly! Love is what the world needs most today. Love does not merely make the world go round – it is what makes the ride worthwhile, as Franklin Jones has said. And true love is love–in–action; for love that does not express itself in action, does not exist at all!

There are very many wealthy people who speak harsh words to the people they serve. They may give a poor man money and tell him, "Don't show your dirty face to me again!" or they may lose their temper and yell, "Don't be so lazy! Don't expect me to prop you up all the time!"

Friends, this is not true service. The people we seek to serve are not apart from us – they are a part of us. This sense of identification is very essential for true service. When you serve others, you must identify with them.

I am told that a tree called the *Upas* tree grows in certain parts of Indonesia. It grows very thick and it secretes poison so that all forms of vegetation around it are killed. There are people like the *Upas* tree – they criticise, condemn others; but will not lift a finger to help others improve themselves.

I read about a fashionable, rich young woman, who was taken around a poor locality of New York City. She was disgusted at the sight of the shabbily dressed, unkempt children on the streets.

"Look at these dreadful children!" she sneered. "Why can't some one wash and clean them up? Do they have no mothers?"

Her guide explained to her patiently, "Sure, they have mothers who love them: but they don't hate the dirt. You hate the dirt: but you don't love these children. Until love for the children and hatred for their condition are found together in the same heart, the children will probably have to remain as they are!"

4. Serve Unconditionally

The fourth principle of service is: Serve Unconditionally! Service should not become interference. If you wish to reform the world, begin with yourself. A true server realises that he must mend his own life, before he begins to set others right.

Many people take to service with an ulterior motive; their service comes with strings attached. They expect the beneficiaries of their generosity to follow their ideology, their beliefs or subscribe to their way of thinking. It is said that some service organisations even try to convert people to their religion, in lieu of services rendered. This is surely inimical to the spirit of true service, which, at its best must be spontaneous, unconditional. Jesus would never countenance our service as an offering to him if we insisted on serving only Christians. Krishna would not accept our service if we offered it only to Hindus. Service should be a labour of love; and love knows no barriers of caste, creed, race or religion.

Aristotle was taking a stroll, accompanied by a few friends. They were accosted by a poor man, who appealed to them for charity. The man was known to have a bad reputation.

Aristotle gave alms to the poor man. This met with the disapproval of his friends.

"You should not have helped him," observed one of them. "You know his reputation. Why do you encourage such people?"

"I did not offer my charity to the man," explained the great philosopher. "I gave it to humanity."

Who are we to judge the worth of needy ones?

This noble spirit of serving without judgement, serving without interference, serving unconditionally was beautifully exemplified in the life of my Beloved Master, Sadhu Vaswani. He once said:

> If I meet a hungry man, let me not ask why he is hungry, when so many others feast at their banquet tables. Let me give him food to eat.
> If I meet a naked man, let me not ask why he shivers in the cold of wintry nights, when so many have their wardrobes filled to over flowing. Let me give him garments to wear.
> And if I meet a man lost in sin let me not ask why he is lost, but with a look of compassion, with a song or a syllable of love, let me draw the sinner to the Spirit.
> Let me draw by awakening the longing that lies latent in all.
> Let me lead some out of darkness into Light!

"Blessed are those who give without remembering: and take without forgetting," says a wise statement.

5. Cultivate the Soul

The fifth principle of service is: If you would serve aright, Cultivate the Soul! Cultivate the soul! Therefore, know that you are only a tool, an instrument. God is the One Worker. Cultivate the Soul! Therefore, do not confound the means with the end. Renouncing all egoism and selfishness, become instruments of the eternal *shakti* that shapes the lives of individuals and nations.

The essence of Vedanta may be summed up in the one concept: All Life Is One. If such oneness is accepted, the question arises, who is serving whom?

The concept of oneness does not take away from the ideal of service. When a speck of dust enters the eye, does the hand not rush to soothe the eye? So too, do human beings help one another, even while they are aspects of the One Life Supreme.

Hindu philosophy teaches us that our true self is the *Atman*, the spirit. The body is just the garment we wear, while we are upon this earth. Thus all activity is work done for the sake of work. For the pious and the devout, all work is an offering to God. All work is His work. You and I are only instruments of God.

This is beautifully expressed in the prayer of St. Francis of Assisi:

> Lord, make me an instrument of Thy Peace,
> Where there is hatred, let me sow love;
> Where there is injury, pardon;
> Where there is doubt, faith;
> Where there is despair, hope;
> Where there is darkness, light;
> Where there is sadness, joy.
> O Divine Master, grant that I may not so much seek
> To be consoled as to console;
> To be understood as to understand;
> To be loved as to love;
> For it is in giving that we receive;
> It is in pardoning that we are pardoned;
> It is in dying to self that we are born to eternal life.

Gurudev Sadhu Vaswani always emphasised the spiritual value of service. For, he believed that the soul stagnates in idleness, even as fresh water grows foul without motion. But he also believed that true service should express love: love for the world around us, the people, birds, animals, and all aspects of creation. For out of such love is true service born.

Talking of *Karmayoga*, Gurudev Sadhu Vaswani teaches us to worship God through service. He also points out the stages in this worship:

1) Offer your service as a duty. Do your work as a disciplined soldier. Do it as your duty. Think not of the fruits of action.

2) Work for the welfare of the world. Look around you! The world is in suffering: the world needs helpers. Serve and be ready to suffer in service of suffering humanity.

3) Work as *yagna*: an offering to God. Dedicate your life to God. If your life is not a dedication to the Divine Life, it becomes disintegration. The life dedicated to the Divine is indeed, a happy life. It is a life of true service: and through it we grow in reverence for the poor, realising that service of the poor is real worship of God.

Thus does service become a prayer. For to serve is to pray. You no more think of "doing good to others". Your service becomes disinterested devotion to the Lord.

• • • • • • • • •

Many people say that this material world of ours is a prison, and the only thing to do here is to escape as best we can. But, let me say to you, this world is what you make of it. Do not forget for a moment, that it is through this human birth that you can attain to freedom. Each one of us has been given the golden opportunity of the human birth, which is, itself, a gateway to freedom, emancipation and liberation. It is for us to choose between making this world a prison, or a gateway to liberation.

J.P. Vaswani

• • • • • • • •

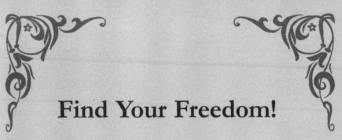

Find Your Freedom!

There were three men, all of them given to excessive drinking. One night, after a heavy bout of drinking they wandered off to a beach. Here, they spotted a boat at the jetty.

"Why don't we take a boat ride," suggested one of the alcoholics. His friends readily agreed. They climbed into the boat and began to paddle. Throughout the night, they paddled the boat. They were tired and exhausted. In their drunken state, they felt that they had sailed miles and miles into the sea. But in the morning, as the sun rose, they looked around and found that they had not moved even an inch. They were still on the beach, at the very same spot from where they had started. The boat was firmly hooked on to the jetty. In other words the boat was bound fast and strong.

Man's condition is similar to that of the drunkards, who paddled throughout the night, without unlatching, unbinding and unhooking the boat.

Free yourself! Unhitch yourself from the world of *maya*. Be unbound, and feel the supreme joy of freedom.

MAKE THE MOST OF YOUR LIFE!

Let me share with you, a beautiful prayer in the words of my Gurudev, Sadhu Vaswani:

Far away from you, I have wandered.
Show me the way, shower your Grace on me.
Wherever I am, wherever I may be, whatever I may do,
In every thought, in every word, keep me close to your heart!
A wanderer can never be happy. A vagabond can never experience stillness.

Are we not, all of us, vagabonds and wanderers?

Birth after birth have we wandered. Lifetime after lifetime, one *janma* after another have we inhabited this world of illusion, as vagabonds from one incarnation to another. And the wandering still continues.

> **The test of true courage is to live well, not to die well.**
> *—Anon.*

What is the root cause of this wandering? It is alienation from God, separateness from the source of all life. We keep ourselves apart from God, the creator of this universe. How can the lotus bloom without water? How can the *rajanigandha* spread its fragrance without moonlight? How can man ever be happy without God?

When you look for happiness, you are not likely to find it. When you lose yourself, you find the Beloved, you find the Lord Himself. You realise then that true happiness is in self realisation.

This miracle will happen in your life too, when you accept the will of God. Whatever you do, whatever you aspire, should be in tune with the Divine Will. Therefore, make this the *mantra* of your life. 'Not my will but Thy Will be done, Lord'. In every circumstance, in every situation, during every crisis, every trauma, accept the Will of God! This will not only open for you the gateway to God's kingdom; it will also lead you to the bliss and peace of heaven on earth.

> **The mind is its own place; and in itself, can make a heaven of hell, A hell of heaven.**
> *—John Milton*

It is with good reason that the spiritual path is described as a tough and demanding one, while the worldly path of the unthinking, unawakened human being is referred to as "the primrose path of dalliance". It is far easier to live a life of mindless pleasure, than to cultivate the spirit in quest of liberation! Let me repeat, the spiritual path is difficult. There are many obstacles on the way. Even when you have scaled the heights, there is ever present, a danger of falling off the peak. To remain safe and secure in spiritual attainment, one needs the protection of the Guru or the grace of God.

Wah Wah Prabhu! All that has happened has happened for the best; all that happens now is the best that can happen; all that will happen in the future will also be for the best. Whatever God does, whatever He wills can only be good for me! Whatever He will do in the future, will also be for my own good! If we cultivate this spirit of acceptance, sorrow and sufferings will vanish from our lives, and we will discover the peace that surpasses understanding, and the joy that no ending knows!

I have often shared this beautiful prayer with my friends. Let me repeat it to you:

Thou knowest everything, Beloved,
May Thy Will always be done!
In joy and sorrow, my Beloved
May Thy will always be done.

How may we make the most of this life – the gateway that can lead us to the kingdom of God?

Let me offer you a few practical suggestions:

1. Throw out those joy-killers that many people carry about with them all the time. Throw out falsehood, selfishness, hatred, greed and lust.

2. Never think or talk negatively.

3. Fill your heart with love – love for God, love for your fellow men, birds and animals, nature, and of course, yourself!

4. Keep yourself active all the time. Remember, the best and noblest activity is to bring comfort to the comfortless.

5. See the good in everyone. Be blind to the faults of others. Constant complaining and criticising only corrodes your spirit.

6. In everything that you do, pour out the best that is in you. Make your thoughts, words, and actions – indeed make your entire life – an offering at the Lotus Feet of the Lord.

7. Do not allow circumstances and your own desires to master you. Rather, aim to be a master over circumstances and your own animal appetites and desires.

8. Let go, let go, let God! Let go of everything. Let God take charge of your life and affairs. Letting go permits divine ideas to flow, divine power to work, divine order to bless your body, mind, soul and your activities.

> **As a tale, so is life; not how long it is, but how good it is, is what matters.**
> *–Seneca*

Life can be changed; life must be changed for the better. Just think of joy, peace, purity, love, perfection and prosperity – and your environment will shape itself in accordance with your persistent thinking. You will find that you need not take the trouble to go to heaven; your life upon earth will become a heaven for you and those around you!

Happiness belongs to those who are immersed in the faith that God can never fail us. In all that happens to us, in all the incidents and accidents of life, there is a meaning of His Mercy, if only we could be tuned to His will. The Great Universe has a perfect scheme of things and whatever happens, has a meaning and a purpose, which is good for us. We should accept the Divine Will, and look upon all that happens to us as *prasad* from God! Such an attitude can be cultivated by praying to God, in the words of Sadhu Vaswani:

> Keep me close to your heart,
> Let me not wander,
> In joy and in sorrow,
> Thy Will, not mine, be done!

About The Author

Born on August 2, 1918, Dada J. P. Vaswani is, indeed, a man in a million or a "smile - millionaire" as admirers refer to him. Scientist and philosopher, humanitarian and teacher, eminent scholar and modern day saint, he is acknowledged as the spiritual leader of millions of Sindhis worldwide.

Utter simplicity, genuine humility, profound wisdom, deep insight into men and matters, wide scholarship, a brilliant analytical mind and tremendous positive faith – all this goes into the magnetic personality that is Dada J. P. vaswani. Over and above all this there is his spiritual power, the mantle that he has inherited from his uncle and mentor, Sadhu Vaswani– a spiritual and intellectual giant of modern India.

Dada J. P. Vaswani's life reflects the richness and multifaceted nature of his personality. After a brilliant academic career, he won a prestigious Fellowship to complete his M.Sc. degree from the D.J. Sind College, Karachi. He had the distinction of having his thesis examined by Sir C. V. Raman. His academic excellence stood him in good stead, as he carved out a distinguished career much later, as Principal of St. Mira's College For Girls – this, no ordinary academic institution, but a temple of learning founded upon the lofty ideals of sympathy, service, purity and prayer and committed to providing a system of value-based education that seeks to integrate intellect, emotion and spirit.

Dada has been the editor of several periodicals, notable among them being *The Excelsior, The India Digest* and *The East and West Series*. Today, he is a highly respected and gifted writer whose books have been translated into many world languages, and run into multiple editions.

He is a brilliant and powerful orator, who has addressed several distinguished international audiences from prestigious platforms such as the World Parliament of Religions, Global Forum for Spiritual Leaders and Parliamentarians, World Hindu Conferences, and Conferences on World Religions. Wherever he speaks – be it at the U.N. or the House of Commons, London, at Chicago, Oxford or Kyoto, Dada J.P. Vaswani has the amazing capacity to captivate and mesmerize his listeners with his fluent language, his logical reasoning, his profound ideas, his practical wisdom – and his gorgeous sense of humour!

Dada is also an excellent administrator. The Sadhu Vaswani Mission which is today a world renowned humanitarian service organization, owes its successful and smooth functioning entirely to his inspirational leadership. Its activities include such diverse areas as education, village upliftment, relief and rehabilitation, medical aid, free housing projects and self-help schemes. The prestigious Sadhu Vaswani Mission's Medical Complex in Pune, includes the Inlaks and Budhrani Hospital, the Morbai Naraindas Budhrani Cancer Institute, the K. K. Eye Institute and the Fabiani and Budhrani Heart Institute. There are no less than nine Mira Institutions in India where over 7000 students receive education from the pre-primary to the post graduate level. The Mission's multifarious departments and activities, and the donations which pour in from generous devotees for the upkeep of these various activities, make the Sadhu Vaswani Mission one of India's most admired and respected Charitable Trusts – and every aspect of these activities is personally monitored under the benevolent leadership of Dada J. P. Vaswani.

Truly, Dada is in the world and yet not of it! The very personification of love and compassion, he is also the repository of practical wisdom; profoundly spiritual and deeply faithful, his tolerance and understanding are remarkable. Indeed, his life's mission has been to spread the sunshine of joy, love, peace and universal brotherhood. Listening to him is an experience of a lifetime – for he makes a remarkable impression upon his listeners.

In April, 1998, Dada was given the prestigious U-Thant Peace Award for his dedicated service to the cause of world peace. This is an indication of the recognition that the world is giving to him and his message – the message of his Master which synthesises past and present, science and spirituality. Dada's mission of spreading his Master's message, has taken him to the four corners of the globe – and wherever he goes, people have responded spontaneously and overwhelmingly to his message of Love and Peace.

Dada's humanitarian spirit transcends caste, creed, colour and religion. His life reflects the essence of the Gita as well as the Sermon on the Mount. The range and extent of his intellect are truly remarkable; he can speak to us on life after death – and on the secrets of an exciting life! He can teach us how to confront problems and challenges– or give us his vision of a world without wars. Abstract speculation and forbidding prohibitions are not for him – he is practical and down-to-earth and communicates effortlessly with his audiences.

Dada is one of those remarkable men whose life is their message; an inspiring teacher who teaches by personal example, an embodiment of love and compassion. His reassuring presence blazes forth the comforting message of the Gita: "All is well, all was well, all will ever be well both now and a hundred years hence!"